To Günzl
with love

D0531847

December 1979

# Passions & Prejudices

## by Leo Rosten

THE POWER OF POSITIVE NONSENSE
O K*A*P*L*A*N! MY K*A*P*L*A*N!
THE 3:10 TO ANYWHERE
THE LOOK BOOK (ed.)
A NEW GUIDE AND ALMANAC TO THE RELIGIONS
OF AMERICA (ed.)
DEAR "HERM"
LEO ROSTEN'S TREASURY OF JEWISH QUOTATIONS
ROME WASN'T BURNED IN A DAY:
The Mischief of Language
PEOPLE I HAVE LOVED, KNOWN OR ADMIRED
A TRUMPET FOR REASON
THE JOYS OF YIDDISH
A MOST PRIVATE INTRIGUE
THE MANY WORLDS OF LEO ROSTEN
CAPTAIN NEWMAN, M.D.
RELIGIONS IN AMERICA (ed.)
THE STORY BEHIND THE PAINTING
THE RETURN OF H*Y*M*A*N K*A*P*L*A*N
A GUIDE TO THE RELIGIONS OF AMERICA (ed.)
THE DARK CORNER
SLEEP, MY LOVE
112 GRIPES ABOUT THE FRENCH (War Department)
HOLLYWOOD: The Movie Colony, The Movie Makers
DATELINE: EUROPE
THE STRANGEST PLACES
THE WASHINGTON CORRESPONDENTS
THE EDUCATION OF H*Y*M*A*N K*A*P*L*A*N

# Passions & Prejudices

## Or, Some of My Best Friends Are People

## LEO ROSTEN

McGraw-Hill Book Company

New York     St. Louis     San Francisco     London
Mexico     Sydney     Toronto     Düsseldorf

Book design by Sallie Baldwin.

1 2 3 4 5 6 7 8 9 0 B P B P 7 8 3 2 1 0 9 8


Library of Congress Cataloging in Publication Data

Rosten, Leo Calvin, date
Passions and prejudices.
I. Title.
PS3535.07577P3      818'.5'207      77–16562
ISBN 0–07–053984–7

*To*
*ZIMI*
once more,
with love

# Contents

# Passions & Prejudices

# 1

## CREDO

I believe that you can understand people better if you look at them—no matter how old or important or impressive they may be—as if they are children. For most of us never mature; we simply grow taller.

I have learned that everyone—in some small, secret sanctuary of the self—is mad. If we want to stay sane we must moderate our demands—on ourselves and on others. Those who do not understand mercy cannot in the end escape the punishment which waits within ourselves.

I have learned that everyone is lonely, at bottom, and cries to be understood; but we can never entirely understand someone else, no matter how much we want to; and each of us will forever be part stranger—even to those who love us most.

I have learned that the dimensions of suffering, of anguish, of pettiness, resentment, rancor, recrimination, envy, lust, despair exceed our wildest imaginings. I have learned, too, that man's capacity for sacrifice, for devotion and compassion and that most astonishing of all virtues—simple decency—can forever hearten and surprise us.

I have learned that it is the weak who are cruel, and that kindness is to be expected only from the strong.

I have come to believe it not true that "the coward dies a thousand deaths, the brave man only one." I think it is the other way around: it is the brave who die a thousand deaths. For imagination, more than conscience, doth make cowards of us all. Those who do not know fear are not really brave. Courage is the capacity to confront what can be imagined.

I have had to learn that life—so precious, so variable, so honeycombed with richness and delight—is held cheap in the scheme of impersonal events. When a human life is snuffed out in an instant, without meaning, without reason, without justice, how can one deny that all our lives hang by threads of nothing more than luck? A vagrant microbe, an oil slick on the road, an open door, a madman encountered by chance—against these what matters all our painful accumulation of virtue? A leak in a gas line, falling glass, a sudden wave, a driver drunk—against such sheer circumstance what matters a life devoted to knowledge or enriched by nobility? What price compassion, what weight sacrifice?

I cannot escape the awareness that in our last bewildered moment, in this world of beauty and wonder and desire, just before we die, three simple, awful questions cry out from our souls: "Why me? Why now? Why forever?"

There is no answer to death; there is only a rueful accommodation to reality. And what is reality but a fortuitous play of circumstance, indifferent to our hopes or our unutterable aspirations? And what is wisdom but the capacity to confront intolerable ideas with equanimity?

I have come to see that every person is subject to fantasies so obscene, yearnings so mendacious, drives so destructive that even to mention them shakes the gates we have erected against the barbarian within.

Nothing in nature, not the glories of the firmament nor the enigmas of the atom, is half so strange as our unconscious—that hidden, heaving sea of primordial impulse in which the most confounding contradictions beat side by side: the insatiable hunger for love, the boundless rage to kill; the clamorous Now, preserved from the most distant Then, in scornful obliteration of time; the yearning to be known, the conspiracy to remain unrevealed; the male, the female, their tragic amalgams.... Not Xanthus nor Xanadu, for all its measureless caverns, provides so stupefying a landscape.

I sometimes think there is a dimension beyond the four of experience and Einstein: insight, that fifth dimension which promises to liberate us from bondage to the long, imperfect past.

I have been driven to believe that no despotism is more terrible than the tyranny of neurosis. No punishment is more pitiless, more harsh and cunning and malevolent, than what we inflict upon ourselves. And in my later years, I came to understand that there is no tyranny more vicious than the demands of neurotics. "For some not to be martyrs is martyrdom indeed."

There is an imperialism in virtue, which compels us to acquiesce to those who exploit it. For each of us is a slave to guilt, and acts out lifelong expiation—however disguised, however symbolic.

During wars or disasters, ordinary men can be lifted into a kind of grandeur, because they act for a purpose larger than themselves.

Most men feel cheated if happiness eludes them. But where has it been written that life will be easy, our days untroubled by suffering, our nights unfouled by the beasts within our nature? Where has it been promised that others will treat us justly; that evil will be slain by innocence before the innocent fall to the wicked; that life can ever be free of awful stretches of loneliness and uncertainty and pain? Where, indeed, is it guaranteed that life will at the very least be *fair?*

People debase "the pursuit of happiness" into a narcotic pursuit of "fun." To me, this is demeaning. In this mortal, muddled vale, death stalks freely, anxiety haunts our steps, depression unexpectedly plagues our hours. I would question the sanity of anyone not often torn by despair. Euphoria is the province of lunatics. And those who seek unruffled pleasure can pray for senility, or drown in drugs that pink the senses with elation.

I cannot believe that the purpose of life is to be "happy." I think the purpose of life is to be useful, to be responsible, to be honorable, to be compassionate. It is, above all, to *matter:* to count, to stand for something, to have it make some difference that you lived at all.

And so, before the last "ding-dong of doom," let us come to terms with the fact that we can live only within a series of impermanent approximations, knowing that our dearest hopes may never be fulfilled, that final truths may remain forever unknown to us, that life—so short, so long, so delicious and baffling and horrid and beautiful—holds nothing more precious than the *process* by which, to the fullest limits of which we are capable, we stretch the mind and heart.

I once heard a story about Destiny, a folk-tale handed down the generations by the Jews. . . . Destiny, the story goes, once appeared on a far-away island and summoned three inhabitants before him. "What would you do," asked Destiny, "if I told you that tomorrow this island will be completely inundated by an immense tidal wave?"

The first man, who was a cynic, said, "Why, I would eat, drink, carouse and make love all night long!"

The second man, who was a pagan, said, "I would go to the sacred grove with my loved ones and make sacrifices to the gods and pray without ceasing."

And the third man, who was a rabbi, thought for a while, fearful and troubled, and said, "I would assemble our wisest men and begin at once to study . . . how to live under water."

I never forgot that story.

When our cause seems doomed and the future lost, when despair overwhelms us and the heart is on the edge of breaking, let men summon hope and honor and high resolve in yet one more stubborn affirmation: "Come, let us assemble our wisest men and begin at once to think, to study, to try to learn—even to learn, if we must, how to live under water."

# 2

---

## WHY NOT RENT A CHILD?

Any amateur historian knows that the Hapsburgs, being hemophiliacs, bled profusely. Well, the Rostens are lacrophiliacs—we cry easily. We weep at weddings no less than at wakes; we choke up at class reunions, blubber over birthday cakes, and when Old Glory goes by, our ululating sobs can be heard above the band. I, whom ardent weepers acclaim a gusher, even get a lump in my throat when the 8:09 flight from Omaha hits the runway.... If my ancestors had only gone in for piracy instead of pilpul, our family escutcheon would feature a large, limp handerkerchief on a field of tears. Motto: *Fondre en larmes*, which is French for "To burst into tears."

These confessions may prepare you for the nerve-racking thing that befell me at the railroad depot the day I bade farewell to my youngest, my final daughter. She was going off to college.... All the while her train crawled out of Penn Station, I trotted alongside her window, making funny faces, waving adieu with false aplomb, freezing a brave smile on my lips. She was off to college—college—my winsome child no more.

5

She went off as happy as a lark, which left me as depressed as a snail. Who can blame a man in this condition for heading to the nearest bar? I needed drink to stiffen a soul of mush, and to stare bitterly into space.

Children. "Women make us poets," says de Chazal, "but children make us philosophers." Well, I was no sapient thinker *that* dark day: I was a cornball father with a matzo-ball heart. Gone, gone, I snuffled, were the ordeals-by-fire three children had put me through: measels and tonsils and plaintive cries in the night; overactive thyroids and underactive arithmetic; allergies, asthmas, rashes, glasses; emergency dashes to the vet with a schizophrenic cat, bankrupting trips to the orthodontist for those goddam retainer-braces. Gone, forever gone, were the droolings of infancy, the pawky pangs of puberty, the gluey amours of adolescence.

Floundering in this flood of maudlin recollections, I must have struck the bar with my fist, crying: "Children! Why does any man in his right mind have children?"

"*I* know why," crooned a voice in my ear.

I turned. On the barstool next to mine was a dapper creature to whom I took an instant dislike. A black coat was draped across his shoulders, a black cravat flowed around his collar, a black fedora perched on his head. He was sallow, razor thin, with sleek black sideburns and a waxed mustache whose tips curved upward like the horns of the dread Miura bull. His eyes had no irises. "I could not help overhearing your anguished soliloquy." He gave me a knowing smile that was less smile than grimace. " 'Why do men have children?' Permit me to answer, sir. One: Nature's Blind Biological Drive. Two: to gratify the image of a cherubic duplicate of the self, which is enormously flattering to the ego. Three: because men are shamelessly hoodwinked by friends who have spawned little ones of their own and, in an effort to augment the company which misery loves, propagandize the dubious joys therefrom in the most glutinous misrepresentations of the Priceless Joys of Fatherhood. Are you with me?"

"What's Four?" I asked.

"Oh, Four is the decisive reason: Men have children because their wives 'Want to Have a *Ba*-by.'" His mimicry of a moony female was uncanny.

"Are you," I frostily inquired, "a father?"

He shuddered. "Heaven (excuse the expression) forfend!"

"Then how can you know—"

"The precious pleasures a child provides? Oh, I know them. I am not without eyes and ears, sir. The tousled little tot in the crib, trailing clouds of glory; the toddler murmuring 'Goo-goo' as she nuzzles your neck; the lad scoring the winning basket for dear old Farragut High; the maiden ecstatic before her first prom—acne on her (or her escort's) cheeks....Those are truly golden moments, sir. And my heart bleeds for all who fall victim to them. There is, in fact, only one thing wrong with having kiddies. Bartender: Two more. On me, sir. It is a pleasure."

"What," I asked, "is the 'one thing wrong' with having children?"

"Its irrevocability." He grinned like a wolf. "The permanent, lifelong peonage of parent to chee-ild. It is arbitrary and tyrannical, sir. You can't return an unsatisfactory offspring, can you? You can't exchange it for one more desirable. No returns. No exchanges. Daddy becomes prisoner to the yo-yo his passion begot. He cannot alter the way the genetic dice came up, so he cannot rectify what he sees was a ghastly mistake. He must accept a tyke who looks like an idiot, will model himself on Jerry Lewis, and is headed for a roach-infested pad in Greenwich Village with a mate from Cheesequake, N.J. That is a real town, by the way, not a put-on." Dracula chuckled. "My heart bleeds for the likes of thee. Why, you can't even divorce a child, as you can a repellent wife, to terminate unjust, lifelong servitude. Once that mockingly called 'Bundle of Joy' appears—pfft! You are trapped forever, Papa....Hence my ingenious plan—a boundless boon to the human species. Ah, our libations." He raised his glass. "Skoal!"

My drink was pure gold and fire. My mind was beginning to glow. "What," I asked, "is your 'ingenious plan'?"

"De-*lighted* you ask, sir. Consider. Your country is a monument to free enterprise, is it not? You can buy or rent, say, a car—any model—for an hour, a day, a week, a year. You can similarly acquire or tentatively possess, a samovar or bicycle. Folding chairs or extendable ladders. A tuxedo, a truck. A boat for fishing or a blind for shooting. You, the consumer, reign supreme. How intelligent. How practical. How enlightened. Very well, sir: Why not rent your children?"

He was, I must say, exceptionally deft in putting me back on the stool from which I had fallen.

"Open your *mind,* sir," he beamed. "Eschew tribal inhibitions!" Before my eyes he now flashed a pamphlet, on whose cover was engraved:

### AMERICAN RENT-A-CHILD AGENCY

Rent a kid—any age, any type—for every mood or occasion.

Be a mother—for as long as you like.

Be a father—for as little as you can endure.

All joy! No lasting responsibility! No after-effects!

FREE DELIVERY AND PICKUP SERVICE.

CREDIT CARDS ACCEPTED

RESERVE A CHILD NOW FOR THE HOLIDAYS.

"But this is insane!" I cried.

"Only to foes of reason. My service, sir, is nothing if not sane! It is surely more rational than nature's thoughtless process of procreation, or society's silly sentence of enslavement for a lifetime. *Think,* sir. Do you pine for a curly-haired little blonde in velvet to sit in your lap and blink her lashes adoringly as you read her *Mary Poppins?* We have just the darling for you: Number twenty-three in the catalogue—Betty Lou. Just read that description: 'Sits entranced for as long as you read aloud. Guaranteed to clap her hands at climactic moments.' . . . Or do you yearn to take a little boy fishing? Fine. Here is Tommy— Number thirty-nine: 'A seven-year-old, freckled redhead, two front teeth appealingly missing. We deliver him to you barefooted, with frazzled jeans and a smudge on his cheek.' . . .

Perhaps you prefer football, sir? Why *not?* Number fifty-two comes 'complete with battered helmet and too-large shoulder pads'." The maniac was talking very fast now. "Perhaps a baby to pat your cheek with loving, sticky fingers? Excellent! We have bawlers with sticky fingers in any substance: mustard, mashed potatoes, oatmeal—or any flavor: chocolate, marshmallow, fudge—"

"My God!"

"Let's keep Him out of this, shall we?" My tormentor purred, a black leopard. "Consider That Man's cruel injustices! Barren wives. Maiden aunts. Old maids. Your secretary. Shall *they* forever be denied maternal joys? No, no, a thousand times no! My plan rectifies divine disasters. Take Number forty-three—a sweet four-year-old who *adores* having her hair brushed. Or, just *look* at this category: 'Children to Eat With!' From now on, no one need envy that euphoric Father and Son at Macdonald's. That beaming Mother and Missy at Schrafft's. . . . We provide children with forty varieties of digestive likes or loathings: Ronnie— seventy-two *dotes* on pickles and popcorn. But seventy-three— Sue Anne—*hates* spinach and is guaranteed to put up a fight, when force-fed, at no extra charge. Or Number thirty-five—Billy Boy—a *dandy* lad, eats anything, anytime, because we deliver him to you famished, at a pre-meal deprivation fee of only—"

"Stop!" I cried.

"Soon. Note our Brother and Sister Combinations! Rent them at a ten percent discount. We can give you siblings who love each other or hate each other, as you wish. They punch, jab, pinch, or make faces. You name it, we supply it. Or look here. What a *delicious* group: 'Take a Tot to the Movies!'" He slapped his thigh: I can swear I heard a metallic sound. "Think of it: little shavers who hate Bugs Bunny and hiss at Woody Woodpecker! . . . Perhaps you are a culture lover? Here—numbers ninety through one hundred six—boys and girls specially trained for trips to museums. We cannot, alas, supply youngsters who take Pop Art seriously; every child we've tested laughs out loud at it."

"Mad," I moaned. "You are raving mad!"

"We are *all* mad, sir," he chuckled, "which is precisely why the Rent-a-Kid scheme took five thousand years to be born. Do look at this one, sir. 'Take a child rowing.' Exquisite. We offer unparalleled choices: urchins who (a) sit quietly midship; or (b) rock the boat; or (c) dangle their little hands in the water; or (d) splash you, the rower. Why, for a modest additional fee, our little ones will even fall out of the boat—thus giving you one of the rarest thrills of fatherhood: a rescue, complete with teeth-chattering gratitude. All our Take-a-Child Rowing entries are expert swimmers, of course. They just *pretend* to be drowning. This lets you save them with a mind entirely free of fear—which is certainly not true if your own flesh and blood is thrashing around in Central Park's Basin."

"Enough!" I groaned.

"Scarcely," crooned the Ancient Mariner. "New subject. Have you ever observed the sorrow of a bachelor uncle or spinster aunt at Graduation Exercises? Must *they* be denied parental pride? Nay, sir! We supply adolescents who will 'graduate' from any one of three hundred schools with whom we have made special arrangements. Our merchandise sits right up on the stage, sir! Their names are read aloud, they step up, receive a diploma, are congratulated by the principal. We even supply top grades and sundry honors, for a small extra sum. Our fee is quite reasonable, you will agree, considering the fact that we must split it with educators: fifty bucks for a high-school ceremony, one hundred for college—which includes cap, gown, and plastic Phi Beta Kappa key."

"Bartender!" I shouted.

"He's deaf," the maniac murmured. "Section Six. Do you realize how many American females are just pining to change diapers? We supply bed-wetters at only $3.50 per hour! That may seem steep, but it has become hard to get reliable bed-wetters these days, because of the inroads of Dr. Spock and progressive education. *Our* enuretics come from the backwoods—Kentucky, the Ozarks—where permissive parents have not yet reaped their dehydrated harvest. Their kids—our specialty—will pee on command or your money back."

"Let me out of here!"

"Stay! Are you man or mouse? In your present mood, sir, I wager you are a sucker for small fry whose lips tremble after a fall. Try our Stiff Upper Lippers, just arrived from England. Or perhaps you want an endearing codger to take on a picnic? To the circus? A trip to the zoo? Then study Group Plan B: 'Ten Juveniles for Outings, Treats, and Excursions: mixed ages.' One is guaranteed to get lost!"

I heard myself keening. His bony hand riveted my knee to the stool. "I just want you to savor a few letters from satisfied clients. Here's one from a cynical podiatrist: 'I am a bachelor who never shared his birthday with a child. Now my life is complete. The little girl you sent me lived up to my fondest dreams of how a grateful child ought to act on her father's birthday.' Isn't that *touching?*"

"No!"

"Here's a letter from a misanthropic couple in Sweet Chalybeate, West Virginia, written by Mr. Gruber Malfeasance the day after Christmas: 'My wife and me sure loved the nine-year-old Son-for-the-day you sent us. He bawled like a stuck pig, just as you promised, all the time I played with his electric train.... So we want to put in our order right now for next Christmas. This time we want a little girl, aged six, to play with a dollhouse while laying on her stomach, with her Mary Janes waggling in the air.' "

I pulled away in horror. "But the *children!* Where do you get those poor, exploited children?"

" 'Exploited?' On the contrary, sir! We sublease them from underprivileged homes! As part-time employees for us, they get much better treatment, food, and entertainment than they ever received at home. And think of the income to their unworthy accommodating parents! We pay them in cash, which is nontaxable, even when they are getting government relief! And remember: rented children, unlike real children, knock themselves out to *please* you, sir, the greedy little things want return engagements. They are far more loving than real brats, who need not bother to court or keep your favor.... Remember the immortal words of Ogden Nash." The ghoul got off his stool, removed his black hat, and recited:

"Children aren't happy with nothing to ignore,
And that's what parents were created for."

"Oh, monster, monster!" I blubbered. "Enemy of *love!* A mother's heart, a father's feeling—"

"I, sir?" He looked hurt. "*I* seek to separate love from slavery, which breeds hate. *I* want parenthood to redeem its promises. Take your own present heartbreak. You would be spared it had you just signed up for Special fifty-four: 'See a Youngster Off to School.' One of our most popular items, what with the craze to educate that is sweeping this land. 'See a boy or girl off to the college of your choice! Wave good-bye and go home *happy!* No post-parting depression!' The children—" he looked around the bar, then whispered, "—get off the train at 125th Street, where we meet them, give them twenty bucks, and return them to their unpleasant homes."

I closed my ears to that evil voice. I flung off that bony, horrid hand. "Bartender!" I cried. "Bartender!"

The bartender, a vision of sanity and cheer, appeared across the gleaming counter. "Refill?"

"No! Throw this nut out of here! Right now. *Throw this man out—*"

The bartender blinked his gentle Celtic eyes. "What man?" he asked.

# 3

---

# HOW TO HATE—IN ONE EASY LESSON

I once committed a lecture, to an entirely innocent group of women, on "Pacifism and its Problems." My theme was simple: The human race is plagued by powerful, irrational, intransigent passions; men could not kill each other unless they possessed the *capacity* to hate and the will to slaughter. During a war, each side swiftly invests its killing with high moral purpose. Theologians of every faith, philosophers and psychologists of every bent, know that our tormented species is caught in a ceaseless struggle between good and evil, generosity and greed, love and hate. Men inflict unspeakable horrors upon each other because they hate what they fear, and kill what they hate.

So pacifism, I ruefully concluded, confronts an ancient, tragic, almost insurmountable task: to mobilize reason and compassion against the terrible trio of insecurity, irrationality, and aggression. War, the most hideous of man's acts, has its roots not only in malevolent leaders or ambitious generals, greedy imperialists or arms manufacturers slathering for "war profits," megalomaniacal statesmen or deluded patriots—but in ordinary, decent men and women, who carry within themeslves rages that can be aroused, passions that can be manipulated, emotions that can become so exacerbated that they become unbearable and cry for release— against an enemy.

That was the thrust of my argument.

As soon as my lecture ended, the usual number of survivors came up to pay the usual compliments and ask the usual questions. One pink-cheeked, beaming little dowager, who looked as if she had stepped right off the cover of a Mother's Day candy box, addressed me, with the utmost kindliness: "Any man who goes around saying God's children are capable of the horrid things you described should be stood up against a blank wall and shot dead!"

Off she marched, trailing clouds of sweetness and light and love for her fellow men. (She never even let me ask why the wall had to be blank.)

I think what was wrong with that dear little old lady (as with so many of our young rebels) is that she had never been taught how to hate properly. By "properly" I mean: (a) relevantly; (b) in proportion, fitting the thing or person hated; (c) without blind rage; (d) without guilt. Her love of "mankind" blinded her to her hatred of those who made her uneasy.

Permit me to tell you another experience.

When I was a sophomore at college, I spent many a happy afternoon shooting pool in the common room with a classmate of whom I was fond. He was a tall, pale, freckled redhead who talked a blue streak. His humor was delightful, his ebullience a tonic, and we beguiled each other with adolescent jokes. Once, I asked him what his father did for a living. He chalked his cue, then sighed, "He's a bishop."

"Why, you son of a bishop!"

He chuckled.

"Not new. It's been said before."

I brought my friend to lunch at my fraternity house one day. He was as garrulous and amusing as ever, but my exalted brothers were cold as ice, and acted oddly offended.

That night, the Pooh-Bah of the lodge took me aside. "Please don't bring your friend to lunch here again. It isn't that we're prejudiced. We just don't want Negro guests."

"Negro?" I gulped. "You must be out of your mind! Why, his skin is fairer than yours!"

"He's a Negro," said the Great Stone Face. "His father happens to be a well-known bishop, black as the ace of spades. We all think you ought to spend less time with your friend— and more with us."

After careful thought, I followed his advice—but reversed the equation: I spent more time with the son of the bishop and less with the sons of the bigots to whom I had pledged my troth.

Don't jump to conclusions. I was *not* acting nobly or with any lump-in-the-throat commitment to the brotherhood of man. I simply found the redhead too *interesting* to drop, far more amusing than anyone at the fraternity. I made my choice for selfish reasons.

You see, I believe in discriminating (if not discrimination). I have practiced discriminating all my life. I discriminate against phoneys, bores, boors, snobs, swine, zealots, and liars. I plead guilty to harboring the most staunch prejudices—against people who blow their nose while I am swallowing oysters, for instance, or yak loudly for hours on an airplane, or call me by my first name upon being introduced.

It is because I believe in discriminating that I pity those who don't. They don't gain the rewards of selectivity because they make no distinction between one Catholic or Protestant or Jew (or Mormon or doorman or foreman) and another.

The prejudiced man practices the rankest form of non-discrimination: He hates people he hasn't even met yet. This is the worst possible way of hating—especially when there are so many sound, 100-percent-American reasons for hating, as you shall see.

The bigot is the pawn of his own fears. He has to prop up a shaky ego by blind asservations of his own superiority. He thinks he makes more of himself by making less of others.

I dislike bigots because if they are fools they try to reason, which they murder; and if they are intelligent, they have to rationalize. I also prefer scoundrels to sadists, musicians to Mau Mau types, and psychoanalysts to psychopaths.

As for hate—well, I hate rabble-rousers, regardless of race, color, party, or creed. I hate anyone who hates others enough to want to harm, harass, or kill them. I believe in honest hate, based on sound evidence and reached after careful thought. The bigot, alas, proceeds on fake or flimsy evidence. He is incapable of listening, much less reasoning, much less changing.

Worse than the bigot, in God's eye, is the fanatic. Bigots are often peaceful churchgoers who sing a nifty psalm; fanatics don't have that much sense of humor. Bigots are despicable, but fanatics are dangerous. A bigot's mind is shut—but so, mercifully, may be his mouth. A fanatic can't shut up. Bigotry is a disease of the soul; fanaticism is lunacy with a program. Scratch a bigot, and you uncover fear; scratch a fanatic, and you uncover rage.

I admit that I am not a top-notch, expert hater because I am a sissy about violence, even in feeling. I compromise my principles by only *wishing* that certain people would drop dead. Nikita Khrushchev, for instance: I detested him as an ignorant, dangerous lout even during his gaudy hadj to Iowa's cornfields, when the American press, acting like schoolgirls, made him out to be a cute and cuddly Slavic uncle. Or Mao Tse-tung. I wanted him to drop dead, too, because he was able, closed-minded, and cold-blooded. I would cheer a coronary on Fidel Castro, who is a liar, a demagogue, and a paranoiac. I would gladly send flowers to any psychiatric ward that incarcerated Colonel Amin of Uganda. I could, if pressed, extend this list to the length of the arm of Kareem Abdul-Jabbar.

But hatred palls, except on the paranoid; let discrimination possess us instead. You have a perfectly proper right to choose whom you want to associate with, or have in your home. But you cannot defend discrimination in public places or tax-supported institutions. Discrimination is a matter of private privilege, not public policy.

I hold no grudge against those who don't want me in their clubs. Most private clubs are dandy places for the kind of people I don't like to spend time with. I loathe locker-room vulgarity and "socials" where camaraderie is expressed by getting drunk and making a pass at someone else's wife. My friend Groucho Marx reduced snobbery to a nutshell by resigning from a country club in these words: "I do not wish to belong to the kind of club that accepts people like me as members."

I once served on a committee that rated candidates for a certain job. We were going through a long list when the name of John B— came up. "Not him," I groaned. "He's stupid."

After the session, a woman came up to me with blazing eyes. "You," she quivered, "...are prejudiced! You ought to be ashamed of yourself!"

"Oh, I am," I replied. "But why now?"

"John B—!" she exploded. "How could you talk that way about a Negro?"

"Oh, dear," I cursed. (In moments of stress I enlist steamy Victorian epithets.) "I had forgotten he's a Negro. I was judging him as a man.... He *is* stupid. He would be stupid if he were white—or red or yellow or as green as you look this moment."

Here is a true story about race prejudice I cherish. Shortly after the war ended, Mr. Jones dropped in on his neighbor, Mr. Smith, in Beverly Hills. (Both names are fictional, to protect the guilty.)

"I know that you love living in this community," said Mr. Jones to Mr. Smith, "and that you're as proud of it as all of us are. I'm circulating this petition. I'm sure you'll be happy to sign it. It's an agreement on the part of the residents not to sell property to any except Caucasians."

Mr. Smith thought for a moment. "What about Will Rogers?

He was one of the best-loved men we ever had here, our mayor. He was part Cherokee, part Mongolian."

Jones scoffed. "I'm not talking about people like Will *Rogers!* ... I'm talking about—well, frankly, *how would you like a Negro living next door?*"

"Which one?" asked Smith.

Jones blinked. "I don't get you."

"Which Negro?" Smith repeated. "It would have to be *someone.* A doctor? Lawyer? Musician? Frankly, I'd prefer any of them to the neighbors I now have. They drink—"

"Mr. Smith! Once a Negro gets into an all-white community, property prices go to hell!"

"No, property prices generally *rise* in a nice neighborhood that opens up to Negroes."

"But *in the long run* property values go to hell!" Jones insisted. "You would lose a lot of money!"

"How much?" asked Smith.

"I beg your pardon?"

"How much would I lose?"

"If Negroes begin buying into Beverly Hills," said Jones, "you could lose around twenty-five thousand dollars!"

Smith considered this. "It isn't enough."

"What?"

"It's not enough. You see, I shave every morning. And when I shave, I look in the mirror. So I would have to look at myself every day for the rest of my life and say, 'You sold out your principles for twenty-five thousand dollars.' "

Jones got up angrily.

"Wait," said Smith. "I'm a reasonable man. Let's make a deal. Any man can be bought, if the sum is high enough. I'm willing to be bribed. ... Tell you what: I'll sign your petition—for, say, a million dollars. Do I alarm you? Okay, half a million. I could find a way of salving my conscience. I would contribute a hundred thousand, say, to a worthy cause; that would still leave me a lot of money. Why don't you go to your friends, those who favor this petition, and buy me out? Just pay me half a million for my house. But a mere twenty-five thousand? No, Mr. Jones. Don't put so small a price on my conscience."

White-faced and trembling, Jones left.

The next morning, Smith got a phone call from Jones: "I didn't sleep very well last night, Mr. Smith. I kept thinking about the things you told me and I tossed and turned half the night. Mister, you certainly mixed me up. I'm not sure you're right, but I don't seem able to answer the points you raised. So I've stopped circulating that petition. My name's still on it, because I'm not sure—but because I'm not sure, I'm not going to try to persuade others I'm right. Good-bye."

Where does hate begin? In the womb? As an instinct? During "the trauma of birth?" In the crib? Because of spanking? Frustration? In "bad" homes?

I do not know. Nor does anyone else, really; one or another authority pinpoints one or another source. But the fact that we do not know why and where hate originates in no way invalidates the fact that hate exists, and that it is deep, virulent, and dangerous. (We don't know what electricity is, either.)

No one who has seen a baby scream until its face turns blue would deny that the baby is convulsed by—call it fury, call it rage. Anyone who has watched tots playing together would be foolish to deny their propensity to violence. Where does anger erupt more swiftly than among the very young? Where are impulses more nakedly displayed and more selfishly gratified? Where are baubles more fiercely guarded or greedily seized? Where are blows, kicks, bites, spit, pinches and punches delivered with less hesitation?

The maudlin may praise childhood's "innocence," uttering sugary prattle about the little angels in our midst. But if you will reflect upon your own experience you will, I think, agree it is not heaven but hell that "lies about us in our infancy."

It grieves me to say that, to the best of our knowledge, hate is as much a part of man as hunger. You can no more stop a child from hating than you can stop him from dreaming. So we must each learn how to manage hate, how to channel it, how to use it where hate is justified—and how to teach our children to do these things, too.

To raise children by drumming into their minds that they do not "really" hate is to tell them a fearful lie. To moon benignly to the child who cries, "I *hate* you!" that (at that moment) he does not—not *really*—is to confuse a child about an emotion he really feels, knows he possesses, and cannot avoid harboring.

The opposite of hate, in this context, is not love; it is hypocrisy. And children loathe the mealy-mouthed.

To ask a child to *repress* hate is to play with fire. Modern psychiatry and medicine agree that people who cannot voice their hostilities express them in other ways: eczema, ulcers, migraine, hypertension, constipation, insomnia, impotence, hallucinations, nightmares, suicide. (Look around you.)

Hate concealed is far more dangerous than hate revealed. To try to bury hate is to intensify it. Hate is more virulent, in the long run, when it is closeted rather than confronted. (Those of you who are shuddering at this point, or who recoil from the unpleasant thought of "animal hate," might remember that animals do not hate the way men and women do: animals attack out of instinct or fear; they kill for food or safety—without the vindictive satisfactions that human hate obtains.)

You may retort that we should teach a child to *understand,* and argue that understanding will defuse his hatreds. But is it not true that the more we understand some people, the more we detest them—and should? Ought we to alter our horror and hatred of a Torquemada, a Hitler, a Charles Manson? Not me.

Do you protest, "But they had an unhappy childhood!" Do you cry, "They're *sick,* not bad!"?

But *all* childhood is full of unhappiness, yet few of us become murderers; and, though most sick people are not "bad," *some* sick people are so evil, so monstrous, that they pass the limits of compassion or defense.

You tell me "Love thy neighbor"? What if your neighbor is Jack the Ripper?

You say "turn the other cheek"? Turn it, if you will, if only *your* life and nightmares are at stake; but would you turn the cheek of a little girl or boy about to be gagged, abused, irreparably damaged by a pervert?

Please notice: In a psychology seminar, I would try to analyze the reasons for A's cruelty or B's greed; in a sociology class, I would place C's delusions or D's hostilities in the larger context of political-social-economic pressures; in a psychiatric clinic, I would seek enlightenment on the unconscious drives, the thwarted hungers, the symbolic function served by X's madness or Y's paranoia.

But in my capacity as a human being, as a living, hurtable mortal, as a member of the human community that must live together in this neighborhood-village-city-country-continent-world—in *that* capacity, can I react to evil except with the most profound moral outrage?

I see no reason to hate sadists less because we understand sadism more. (You may remember the couple in England who tape-recorded the screams of the children they tortured, then murdered. They were psychopaths, to be sure; and to be equally sure, they committed unspeakable horrors—which they enjoyed.)

There is a subtler point here: Not *ever* to hate is to surrender a just scale of decent values. Not ever to hate is to drain *love* of its meaning. Not to hate *anyone* is as crazy as to hate everyone.

Besides, a world of automatic, indiscriminate loving is suicidal—for the good and the loving are enslaved or exterminated by those who gratify their cruelty and their lust. A world that has experienced the horrors of ideology rampant in Russia, China, Cambodia, Pakistan, Ireland has reason to know that neither truth nor justice nor compassion can possibly survive unprepared and unarmed.

Blind hatred is, of course, horrid and indefensible. But hate need not be blind. Hate can be clear-eyed—and moral. Hate need not be our master but our servant, for it can be enlisted in the service of decency (hating those who hate decency), of kindness (hating those who choose to be cruel), of love itself (hating those who hate love and seek to corrupt it).

Are you thinking that this violates "our better selves," or betrays our Judeo-Christian precepts? But the Bible tells us: "The bloodthirsty hate the upright" (*Proverbs*). I am not about to parade my uprightness, but I hate the bloodthirsty; and I think the upright *should* hate them. Shall we allow the bloodthirsty to prevail?

There is indeed a time to love and a time to hate, and the Eighty-ninth *Psalm* uses a phrase of transcendent morality: "I hate them with perfect hatred."

I, for one, especially hate political fanatics (whether from the left or right) who are ready to kill me or you or our children with the detestable certainty that they are right.

I hate injustice, therefore I hate those who treat others unjustly (because of their color, or creed, or simply because they are powerless).

I hate those who teach others to hate those who disagree with them: I loathe demagogues.

All these things I would teach our children.

I would not offend their good sense, or nauseate their sensibilities, by glutinous yammerings about indiscriminate love—love that does not brand evil for what it is, that does not respond with moral passion to those who inflict agony or indignities on others. Such love Emerson dismissed with contempt as the love that "pulses and whines."

I hope our children will learn how and whom and when to hate, no less than how and whom and when to help, forgive, or love.

Home is where hate can and should first express itself, and be taught to contain itself, in proper dosages and proportions. Home is where children should be allowed to practice and test and begin to conquer this powerful, terrible human passion.

Home is where it is *safe* to hate—first.

*P.S.* Voltaire, who said more sensible things more astringently than anyone before or after him, once wrote: "Prejudice is the reason of fools." Some wit called prejudice "an opinion that holds a man"; another dubbed it "the divine right of fools."

But the most disturbing comment was Mark Twain's: "I'm quite sure I have no race prejudices. . . . All I care to know is that a man is a human being—that's enough for me: he can't be worse."

# THE GLORIES OF THE PRESS

I have often celebrated the glories of journalism—particularly those stories, from newspapers around the world, that give me immeasurable delight. For novelty, lunacy and surprise, fiction cannot begin to compete with fact. Mark Twain knew why: Fiction has to make sense . . . and life doesn't.

So, I *love* newspapers. I read them with relish—even passion. To me, each morning's paper is a gorgeous "bazaar of wonders and follies, a forum, a college, a freak show, a stage."

The best stories on earth parade through the columns of newsprint: stories with plots beyond what any writer in his senses would dare to contrive—with characters only God, in his infinite variety, could concoct. Where but from the kooky carnival of life could one possibly find a country woman such as the one who entered a hotel elevator, for the first time in her life, and, glancing at her room key ("1263"), cheerfully pushed the buttons numbered 12, 6, and 3?

Or a character such as the European composer who so hated the "illogical" American custom of writing an address by placing the number before the street name that whenever he was in a New York cab, he would maliciously instruct the driver, "Go to number 46."

"Number 46 *what?*"

"Don't worry." The composer grinned evilly. "Just go to number 46, and I'll tell you the name of the street when we get there."

Or the young lady, reported by Norton Mockridge, who filled out her application for Blue Cross this way:

> *Date of Birth:* Jan. 12, 1940
> *Weight:* 6 pounds, 10 ounces
> *Height:* 20 inches

All of these are culled from my excursions through the press. Not mine alone, I should add: I implore my friends to send me sustenance for my vice from wherever they may roam.

The finest headline I ever read was in the old, forever-lamented *Herald-Tribune* of New York:

GIRL SEDUCED ATOP 65-FT. FLAGPOLE

You don't have to be a professor at the Columbia School of Journalism to know that a headline like that is a "stopper." Rarely, in fact, can there have been a stoppier one.

The story was every bit as stopping as the caption. It recounted how a thirty-four-year-old car salesman in El Paso, Texas, was charged with the "statutory rape" of a fifteen-year-old girl he allegedly seduced atop a flagpole that was sixty-five feet high. The hanky-panky took place in this novel locale because the alleged Don Juan was a flagpole-sitter by profession, and he had spent no less than sixty-four days on the flagpole before committing libidinal acrobatics *in situ.*

The girl, whose name the authorities quite properly did not reveal, told the police she had actually been seduced five times —"after climbing a rope ladder to the top of the pole a number of times." The fact that this lass had climbed a sixty-five-foot *rope* ladder "a number of times" (I couldn't climb a twenty-foot aluminum ladder) made me wonder whether the muscular maiden could make the charge of seduction stick. In my opinion, ascending a sixty-five-foot flagpole of your own free will after you have been seduced on each preceding ascension (except the first, of course) is strong prima facie evidence of a not-entirely traumatic experience. It certainly does not smack of forcible entry.

So I read this story with beady-eyed skepticism. I wondered about what physical arrangements, fit for sex, are conceivable, much less probable, on top of a sixty-five-foot flagpole. "Statutory" rape, I know, has nothing to do with statutes—on or off flagpoles; it is merely the legal phrase for sex with girls under a certain age, whose consent to copulation does not count. But on a *flagpole?* ... Was the girl a midget? ... Didn't the batrachian wrastlings send the lovers tumbling down? ... How much pleasure is possible way up in the air on a ball not large enough to play Parcheesi on, much less you-know-what?

The news dispatch shrewdly waited until the third paragraph to tell us that the dastardly flagpole sitter was not actually *sitting* on top of the ball on top of the pole, but reclined on a 4½-by-5-foot wooden platform, suspended from the top.

This revelation annoyed me.

Perhaps the most tantalizing news item I ever read was this one, in *The New York Times:*

> Recently a (borough of) Queens salesman began wondering if he shouldn't consult a psychiatrist. Every time he drove his car, he thought it was raining. He clearly heard the sound of gurgling water, but no rain was falling.

My psychiatric consultant, whom I promptly telephoned with these glad tidings, came up with a nifty explanation of why a salesman in Queens would think he heard water gurgling every time he got into his car:

(1) The man *hated* to go out on the road; so

(2) the rain he imagined hearing was no more than wish-fulfillment; hence

(3) this was a perfectly understandable feat of the sales-

man's unconscious—which, preferring to stay in bed with the salesman, cunningly produced the sounds of rain in an effort to

(4) trick the salesman into going home at once to lie down with a cold towel on his brow.

I did not have the heart to tell my exuberant psychiatrist what the remainder of the story revealed:

> Finally, one day, he (the salesman) listened closely to his steering wheel and headed for the nearest service station. It seemed that the car's steering column was full of water, which had accumulated from both condensation and leakage.
>
> The mechanic told the salesman it was the first time he had ever run into such a problem.

It's the first time *anyone* heard of such a problem, if you ask me, and I'm grateful to the crackerjack reporter who gave me this opportunity to broaden my horizons.

One old acquaintance earned my gratitude by clipping this gem from the *Letters to the Editor* column of a New Delhi journal called *Link:*

> Every man is as much entitled to his own smell as his own color. Do not permit yourselves to be culturally castrated by American imperialists! Let them keep their water and their soap!
>
> *Yours faithfully,*
> S. R. LYSTER

A classmate passing through Calcutta sent me this cutting for the *Amorit Bazaar Patrika:*

> Barbers in China, inspired by the little Red Book, have "revolutionized the work of haircutting to such an extent that the Chinese people have further realized the greatness of Chairman Mao's Thoughts," according to a New China News Agency report.
>
> In a leading town of Hunan, a group of barbers found

that they had not "served the people" in conformity with Chairman Mao's Thoughts. They had been "unconsciously influenced by the remnants of capitalist thoughts"—for whenever customers walked into their shops, they used to judge them by their attire. Those who looked prosperous always got the best service.

But now, enlightened by Chairman Mao's Thoughts, the barbers look upon such errors with disgust! To redeem themselves, they make a point of *serving the poor customers first*. Those in tattered clothes or rags are given priority.

If this won't convert you to Communism, I guess nothing will. A Las Vegas paper once ran this ad:

*Wedding Gowns for All Occasions*

—which ranks in my memory with the Hong Kong tailor who promised:

Customers giving orders will be instantly executed

Perhaps the most delectable story I ever read was this one, in London's *Telegraph:*

A man who removed a stuffed tiger from a zoo's publicity display at Waterloo Station got no farther with it than the taxi rank.

The police arrived as he was trying to get into a taxi-cab with the stuffed animal, with the help of the driver and a porter. The tiger, a rare Sumatran specimen valued at £500, was too big to go into the vehicle.

At Croyden Crown Court, Samuel William Smith, 50, was found not guilty of stealing the tiger. Smith told the court that while he was looking at the display, a youth told him he could have the tiger for £35. "He said that as the exhibition was closing that night, the stuffed animals were for sale cheaply.

"I thought it was a bargain at the price; but because he was so young, I hesitated. He suggested I phone Chessington Zoo for confirmation, and wrote down the zoo's phone number.

"I went straight to a kiosk and rang the number. A man replied: 'Zoo. Can I help you?' I said I was interested in buying the tiger in Waterloo Station and could he confirm that the price was £35? He did.

"A railway policeman came to the taxi and asked me where I was taking the tiger. I said I was taking it home to my wife. He arrested me for taking the animal without permission of the rightful owners."

Smith told the court he now believed he had been hoaxed. "The phone number the youth gave me must be that of another phone box right in Waterloo Station."

One of the endearing characteristics of the English press is the deadpan with which the papers report outlandish events. For example:

In Kirby Misperton, England, zoo officials paid out more than £280 to visitors last year for articles stolen from them by monkeys.

The monkeys specialize in snatching eye-glasses from the wearers' noses when visitors bend forward to make out a sign on the cage. The sign reads: WARNING—THESE MONKEYS SNATCH GLASSES

Or take this headline:

GOLDFISH SAVED FROM DROWNING

The story revealed that the Royal Society for the Prevention of Cruelty to Animals had recommended that a proper award be given to one Peter Humphrey "for saving a goldfish from drowning." How this marine miracle was accomplished is described in these words:

Mr. Humphrey discovered the goldfish gasping for air on the surface of his garden pond at Hillside Crescent, Uxbridge. He fished it out and found its mouth was jammed open by a pebble. Gently he went to work and gradually eased the pebble out. Then he put the fish back into the water, where it quickly recovered.

Tonight Mr. Peter Hume, an R.S.P.C.A. inspector, said: "Mr. Humphrey's prompt action undoubtedly saved the fish's life. I will be preparing a report to be put before the Awards Committee. There are not many people who know that a fish could drown if it swallows too much water. I hate to think how many goldfish owners have stood by and let a fish drown because they did not know what was wrong."'

The thought makes me shudder, too.

How can I express my gratitude to the London columnist who gave this next news item to a hard-pressed world?

A young British surgeon, on his first visit to America, was invited to look up a cystoscope (an instrument for viewing the inside of the bladder). To his astonishment, he saw the sign:

VISIT JOE'S BAR

For a moment the young surgeon thought he was beholding the final extremity of a national mania for advertisement. Then he moved the instrument, and saw that he was gazing at a segment of a plastic cocktail stick.

How it got there remains a mystery.

The Iron Curtain, of course, strangles levity in matters political, but the famous Moscow *Krokodil,* a weekly virtuoso of satire, did print this apocryphal item under HELP WANTED:

Typist. To copy Top Secret documents. Must be unable to read.

The staid *Christian Science Monitor* once reported, of a western resort town:

This place is known as the preferred resort of those wanting solitude. People searching for solitude are, in fact, flocking here from all corners of the globe.

That lulu of logic reminds me of Yogi Berra's comment on a famous Broadway restaurant: "That place has become so crowded that no one goes there anymore."

And from tormented Greece, not long ago, I read a dispatch that contained this joke, making the rounds of Athens:

> At a meeting between the Greek Premier and the Chinese Communist leader, Mao Tse-tung, the latter asked how many people there are in Greece.
>
> "Eight million," the Premier replied.
>
> "Really," said Chairman Mao. "And what hotel are they staying at?"

*     *     *     *     *

Sometimes the information I get from the press strikes me as so far-fetched that I wonder whether I'm having my leg pulled, or whether the reporter's informant was having *his* leg elongated.

Take the story, on the fashions page of a respectable daily, that celebrated men's mufflers "made of shahtoosh." Now I've read a great many English words since I was a lad, but never have I run across "shahtoosh," or any reasonable facsimile thereof. I consulted three dictionaries and found nary a mention of "shahtoosh." Nor will you. Fortunately the story went on to edify us all:

> Shahtoosh is considered, at least by Texans, the most precious fiber in the world. The goats who go leaping among the Himalayas leave a few hairs from their chins on brambly bushes from which they nibble leaves. Then women come along and pick off the hairs and weave them into a gossamer fabric that is even softer and finer than vicuña. Its muted honey-beige color is almost identical. A muffler made of (shahtoosh) is priced at $125.

I don't think that $125 is at all unreasonable for Texans to pay for mufflers woven out of goats' chin-hairs plucked from bushes in the Himalayas. Why, I spent eight dollars for a muffler made of the wool from lazy lambs who were probably lying around, on unemployment relief, in a meadow near Tenafly, New Jersey, baaing and babbling about their dreary life-style. I think it's worth 125 clams just to be able to drop the word "shahtoosh" into a conversation—because you can bet your boots that some patsy will ask, "What was that you said your muffler is made of?"

"Shahtoosh," you can answer with a world-weary air.

When asked what in hell "shahtoosh" is, you can say, "It's a gossamer fabric woven by Himalayan natives who collect the chin-hairs of goats..." No, you'd better drop the whole *megilla*, lest you become a pariah for the rest of the social season.

The most frustrating newspaper story is the one that gives you crisp, lean facts without a word of explanation—when explanation is the very *sine qua non* of the matter. Take this infuriating paragraph, which appeared under a photograph of a dazed man and woman in their forties:

### SELLING HOME TO PAY PHONE BILL

Mr. and Mrs. James Young ponder their problem in Mission Hills, California—a telephone bill of $4,509.81. Their nineteen-year-old daughter called her sailor husband on Adak, an Aleutian Island, ninety-five times in thirty-eight days. Their $27,000 home is for sale so they can pay the bill.

That's the whole item as printed. I can't begin to tell you how much that story irritated me. For the rest of that day I pestered myself with possible answers to the questions imbedded in and provoked by the dispatch:

Didn't Mr. and Mrs. Young *know* what their nineteen-year-old daughter was up to? Did they ever caution, admonish, whack, or otherwise chide her? Did they *approve* of a nineteen-year-old magpie telephoning the Aleutian Islands as often as three times a night? Were they—well, ambivalent? Were they hostile? Were they engaging in some clever entrapment? Were they now selling their home because they thought it's worth selling your homestead so that your darling chatterbox can talk to a sailor ninety-five times in thirty-eight days? Do they approve of *anyone* talking to anyone on the phone ninety-five times in thirty-eight days? Were they, like Hamlet, nuts—or just pretending to be nuts? Did they never once get on the line to say "Hello, son. How are things in Adak?" or "Hang up, goddammit, or we'll have to sell our house to pay for these idiotic calls!"?

Things like this make you question the whole American way of life. Should any of my readers happen to live in or near Mission Hills, California, please contact Mr. and Mrs. James Young. Find out what they're doing. Find out what their daughter is doing. Find out if they have a new phone. Don't give me the number.

Sometimes a run-of-the-mill news item contains profound sociological implication. Take a story I read in Rome, captioned:

VENICE AREA SHOWS RISE IN BIRTHS
NINE MONTHS AFTER BLACKOUT

The story was welcome confirmation of the theory, long held by sensible demographers, that in any country there is an inverse correlation between the birth rate and the electricity supply: *i.e.,* the more electricity, the lower the birth rate; the less light, the more babies. The reason should be obvious to anyone over twenty lucky enough to have had all the lights go off at night whilst with a comely female—anyone, I mean, who didn't have to wonder how to spend the rest of such a fortuitous evening.

In the Venice area, exceptionally high tides in the Adriatic flooded Venice, Rovigo, and other towns, and immobilized the dynamos that generate electricity. Nine months later the birth rate soared fifteen to forty-five percent.

The same copulatory correlation manifested itself in New York City after the celebrated power blackout on November 6, 1965. (It was my luck to be in a swimming pool in a hotel basement, at the time—alone, alas.) I give you the summary of that historic night that appeared in the *Times:*

A sampling of New York City hospitals precisely 274 days (about the mean between the minimum and maximum gestation period) after the blackout, showed birthrate increases ranging from thirty-six to fifty-five per cent.

The way I interpret this is not that New Yorkers are either more lascivious or fecund than Italians (remember that the increased birth rate around Venice reached only forty-five percent) but that:

(1) the Italian birth rate, to begin with, is higher than the New York birth rate, hence, any increases in babies would be proportionately smaller;

(2) Italians are more accustomed than New Yorkers to having all their lights blow out.

I give you both interpretations with regret.

\* \* \* \*

Since newspaper stories vary in length, the space remaining in a column of print must be filled out with a brief item. These "fillers" are among the most enchanting baubles of information I know. It was from such "fillers," in the newspapers of Chicago, Los Angeles and New York, that I learned such astonishing, if not memorable, things as these:

- In Burma there are deer that bark. (Whether they bark in Burmese, I do not know.)
- Peter the Great kept a large glass vase in his bedroom—containing the pickled head of a mistress who had fallen out of royal favor.
- The quail is both monogamous and polygamous.
- Whenever Lord Palmerston visited Queen Victoria for a weekend, at Windsor or Balmoral, all the royal ladies-in-waiting double-bolted their doors, night after night—so raunchy was Palmerston's concupiscence.
- In Orissa, India, natives (of the Junag tribe) sleep in the open, *underneath* their raised, comfortable houses. These houses are built on stilts—and are occupied by the natives' goats.

- The saliva of bats prevents blood from coagulating—so when a bat punctures the skin of a horse, cow or goat (bats *rarely* nick humans), the blood continues to flow freely.

- Antidotes, according to some unnamed sixth-grader, is what one should take to kill dotes.

- A Boston book review contained this immortal line, "I have no doubt that this book will fill a much-needed void."

If for no other capture of gorgeous trivia, I am in debt to the press for informing me about the Kentucky farmer who went to the theater for the first time in his life, in Louisville. The program read:

Act 1—The Chapin home.
Act 2—One night later.
Act 3—The courtroom.

The farmer left after act one. He returned, believe it or not, one night later.

And a lady who sternly forbids me to reveal her name airmailed the following pearl from some paper whose name she could not decipher:

A hardy explorer was describing—endlessly—his trek thru the Brazilian jungle to a very bored Ladies' Auxiliary. "There I stood," he said after about an hour, "drinking in this amazing scene, with a giant abyss yawning before me."

The president of the Auxiliary interrupted, "Are you sure the abyss was yawning before you got there?"

It was from a newspaper that I received the intriguing news that a Mrs. Elizabeth Hammond, of Gillette, N.J., owns a pet 900-pound elephant, called Mignon, who sleeps in the living room, turns on the TV when bored, and blinks lamp lights on and off to signal that she is going to sleep.

The neighbors think that Mrs. Hammond is bereft of cranial marbles, but her husband and children have accepted Mignon as just another revelation of the lady's love of animals—which include a pet lion cub, three dogs, a horned owl, a bobcat, and a python twelve feet long.

Mrs. Hammond used to train animals for their debut on the stage of the Metropolitan Opera. She rents her adorable pachyderm out to Republican party clambakes or sales promotion extravaganzas.

Perhaps the most startling aspect of all this *mishegoss* is that Mignon, who was born in Thailand, has developed a passion for roast-beef sandwiches.

And it was in a newspaper advertisement that I read Groucho Marx's blurb for a book by S. J. Perelman:

> From the moment I picked this book up until the moment I put it down, I could not stop laughing. Someday, I hope to read it.

* * * * *

No hymn to the press would be complete without *some* mention of the priceless "typos" (typographical boo-boos) which not even the most finicky proofreaders can prevent. Here are a few of my favorites:

> Miss Carlisle, a budding author, has been circulating her navel among various Hollywood producers.
> —Chicago *Tribune*

> Picking up his hammer and two broads, he returned to the cabin to finish the job.
> —Terre Haute *Tribune*

> Millions of desirable women are unattacked and hungry for love.
> —Omaha *Shopping Guide*

> He desperately clung to the sill by his fingerprints.
> —Chicago *Tribune*

> Beethoven, who had ten children, practised on a spinster in the attic.
> —Philadelphia *Bulletin*

Lapses in editing can be funnier than errors in spelling. Examples:

Underneath those ragged trousers beat a heart of gold.

> —from an obituary in the
> Boston *Globe*

The Fire Department will blow the siren fifteen minutes before the start of every fire.

> —*Wayne County Mail*
> (Ontario, N.Y.)

The driver swerved to avoid missing her husband.

> —Elgin (Ill.) *Courier News*

A girl who is 17 is much more of a woman than a boy who is 17.

> —N.Y. *Journal American*

The baseball game, which was held in Mr. Simpson's cow pasture, ended when a runner slid into what he thought was second base.

> —Some Iowa weekly

He collapsed on the sidewalk and died without medical assistance.

> —N.Y. *Times*

The ball hit him on the right temple and knocked him cold. He was taken to Ford Hospital where X-rays of his head showed nothing.

> —N.Y. *Herald-Tribune*

The jury's verdict showed they were of one mind: temporarily insane.

> —St. Louis *Globe-Democrat*

\* \* \* \* \*

Finally, excruciating prose gives me (once I get over my outrage) as much amusement as delightful "typos." It is hard to believe that the following passages were actually printed in reputable—even distinguished—newspapers:

*There is Richard Burton growling and grousing and endlessly chewing the lips, ears and neck of Elizabeth Taylor as the faithless wife of a dull ambassador, with whom he is having a clandestine affair.*

I am glad, in a way, that Mr. Burton was endlessly chewing the ears and neck of Miss Taylor as the faithless wife of a dull ambassador, because it probably wouldn't be fun to chew her neck as anyone else. But *who* is the ambassador with whom Burton is having a clandestine affair?

*The maintenance of political balance under such circumstances could consume hours of TV time with the total exposure accorded the peripheral candidates actually exceeding the visibility of the two men who realistically are meaningful contenders for the right to control the country's destiny.*

Have you ever heard a camel coming down a flight of iron stairs?

*The first time a man wears a hairpiece, he feels that everyone whom he passes throughout the day is staring at his head. It usually takes a while for him to become accustomed to wearing it.*

To me, it is clear from this observation that a toupéed man does not think he is being stared at:
1) after sunset
2) by pedestrians whom he does not pass—*i.e.*, those beside him or behind him.
3) whilst seated anywhere—on a barstool, on a bus, in a restaurant
The referent of "it" clearly is "head"—but all the people I know took no time at all becoming accustomed to wearing theirs.

*. . . and then, with a grinding musical change of gear that is the albatross around the work's neck, (the ballet) "La Valse" itself, that volcanic tone poem of ballrooms before the lamps went out all over Europe, comes together to give Balanchine a musical fantasy of madness, which he takes and distills into a beautiful, deadly waltz.*

Well, I haven't read much beautiful, deadly prose lately, or distilled any fantasies of madness, but I know one thing: a grinding change of gear can't be an albatross around anyone's neck, even *after* the lamps have been turned on in ballrooms all over Europe.

*He and the curious, creepy soldier that Robert Forster gravitates on tennis shoes, never fully bringing out of the shadows, are the surprise and lurking mystery of the film.*

The real mystery lies not in the film but in the reviewer. If you're going to belabor an actor for gravitating on tennis shoes without fully bringing out of the shadows, you should at least advise him, out of human kindness, how to gravitate so that he does fully bring out of the shadows. He should try bedroom slippers.

*But nobody, neither driver nor taxi user, neither policeman or civic officials, are happy about these latest reforms.*

Well, many people is mighty unhappy about the way such writing clobbers our lovely language.

*What glory is there in wrapping oneself in, or wiping one's feet on, a lifeless specimen of man's dwindling heritage of nature's wild beauty?*

What glory, indeed?

*Beneath the evident bourgeois boredom of the daily rounds on an army base and behind the cliché ritualism of presumably efficient military routine, there is slowly and fearsomely shown the flabby undersides of a clutch of weak grotesques and the cheapness, hypocrisy and cruelty of the wholly self-indulgent way they live.*

The fumblefist who committed that sentence is not my idea of the right fellow to sneer at other people's clichés, given the wholly self-indulgent way he writes.

*But the contours of the Haitians are vivid, from the lithe and lurking killer-police through a range of calm, sincere and volatile rebels right down to a lurid voodoo priest.*

The contours of such lithe and lurking prose would have made the late Dorothy Parker, as she put it, fwow up.

*Among her biggest gambles was during their tempestuous courtship.*

I hate to be a spoilsport, but you can't just "was" during anything.

*These police, who bear some distinct resemblance to certain cadres of bearded and dark-glassed terrorists who have lately been evident in this country, are the outward and visible signs of an inner ill—a political and social snarl of ugly purport— that a prescient person in the community cannot dismiss.*

Well, I know one prescient person who is beginning to show visible signs of an inner ill, and it doesn't come from any snarl of ugly purport. It comes from reading mush like that.

*King Louis XIII . . . ordered a wig to simulate real hair; this was taken as a signal to the court and enough of them were subsequently made to keep 850 Parisian wigmakers in business.*

To what does "them" refer? The court?

*The ending of this present offering is, for example, highly theatrical, and very often his dialogue catches the bleakly despairing tones of people on the brink.*

If you ask me, this *non sequitur* catches the bleakly despairing tones of a man around the bend.

*As a people, Americans have come a long way. . . . Colonial status had developed into nationhood that, in turn, has become international in its outlook.*

I can't figure out how nationhood, which is a condition or state of being, can develop an "outlook." If you must barbarize, gentlemen, be consistent: ". . . nationhood that, in turn, has become internationalhoodistic in its outlook."

*Coda:* The Business Section of the admirable *New York Times* once published advertisements that showed a full-bosomed *tchotchke* in a very skimpy bra and panties leaning forward invitingly. The caption under this photograph read:

HI—I'M EVELYN
and I'm Available
for
Trade Shows
Conventions
Business Meetings

Well, I'd like to run an ad, too. It would show a haggard writer, tears pouring down his cheeks, over this caption:

HI FELLOWS—I'M LEO
and I'm Available
for
Lessons in English

# 5

---

## DANGER: Foreign Tongue!

The guidebooks urge any American venturing abroad to learn the basic phrases of a foreign language. Tourist tip-sheets assure you that natives just adore hearing a visitor roll his tongue around theirs. Well, I hate to say this, but the advice is cockeyed, and if you fall for it, you'll end up up to your armpits in the treacherous quicksands of phonetics.

Suppose you're in Uzbek (that's just an example) and, spying an itinerant Uzbekian, utter a debonair "Hello, Charley!" in Kurdish. That will certainly flatter the most Kurdish of Kurds, but it makes him think you understand his ghoulish lingo; so his eyes light up and he answers you—in a burst of colloquial gibberish. This not only dumfounds an American; it fills him with dismay and shame anent his linguistic inferiority.

No, brave voyager, take my advice: *Never try to speak a foreign tongue*. Speak English. The natives, spotting you for the illiterate you are, will knock themselves out to help you; and their joyous cries and gestures and pigeon-prattle will be oodles easier for you to comprehend than the flapdoodle which would

42

follow your breezy *"Où est le john, frere Jacques?"* or *"Haben Sie ein Autojack?"*

The terrible truth is that the slightest slip in pronouncing one little vowel, in any language, can throw you straight into bedlam. Take English. Our *mama-loshn* is sheer torture for a foreigner to pronounce. The difference between "Call me" and "Kill me," for instance, is only 1/64 of an inch of air space, so a greenhorn in a hurry can wind up being throttled by an American eager to oblige a customer from abroad.

I was once accosted in Washington by a gent in a dashiki who, with a courtly bow and the sweetest of smiles, exclaimed: "Hollow Sarah!" Only quick thinking kept me from defending both my solidity and my manhood: the poor wretch *thought* he was producing the proper noises for "Hello, sir."

Or take a simple, straightforward sentence such as: "I want my meat well-done." Naively uttered by, say, a Papuan, that sentence comes out, "I want my mate walled in." Very few restaurants will brick up your wife on such short notice.

The same booby traps await the Americano who is fool enough to plunge into the jungle of an alien argot. One morning in Paris (pronounced "Paree"), my wife drove the hotel's *concierge* into a squirrel cage when she complained about the feeble amount of heat (the Gauls call it *chauffage*) coming out of our radiator. What Madame Rosten actually *said*, in her revised, unstandard version of French, was: "Attention! Chauffeurs are missing from my radiant editor!"

The *concierge* replied that Madame's radiant editor (me) had ordered a car and chauffeur for 11, and it was now only 7:40.

My wife wailed that she had been shivering with cold since 6:20 and wanted the chauffeur turned up *immédiatement.*

The *concierge* exclaimed that he would telephone the garage at once.

My wife cried: "Stop trying to cut expenses by borrowing a heater from a garage! Just rouse your lazy janitor, who is probably napping, or your greedy superintendent, who goofs off, and turn up the heat—or I shall report you *to the police!*"

The *concierge* promptly phoned a superintendent of the police and demanded he broadcast a search for a chauffeur who had been kidnapped by a lazy janitor.

Semantic snafus like that can just about unhinge you. In Tokyo, I carefully read aloud (from a phrase-book called *You, Too, Can Speak Japanese*) the phonetic syllables for "I—would—like—a—massage." To this the Oriental attendant replied, with ceremonial hisses of joy and abnegation: "I would be honored to carry you there on my back, exalted thimble, but the cat is already late for the wedding."

I think I had misled him. Either that, or he was relying on his vest-pocket copy of *You, Too, Can Spoke Engrish.*

Occidental places can be just as disorienting. I once entered a splashy men's store in Madrid and, in buoyant high-school Spanish, informed the clerk that I wanted to purchase a pair of gloves and an umbrella. The oaf turned white, whinnied and dashed off, bleating for his superior.

To this person in a morning-coat and striped trousers, I calmly repeated: "I want—a—pair—of—men's—gloves—and an umbrella."

The superior Iberian flinched. ""But, *señor*," he quavered, "why do you wish to wallop yon horse with a parachute?" Oh, it was jolly.

What happened, as I reconstruct the linguistic mish-mosh, was this: the Spanish for umbrella is *paraguas*, which I mangled into *paracas*, which they took to mean *paracaídas*, which means parachute. Gentleman is *caballero*, which I blithely rendered as *caballo*, which means horse. It was a cinch to nose-dive from *guante* (glove) to *guantada* (wallop), even though I have never laid a glove on a horse, much less walloped one with a parachute. I have never even chastised a Chihuahua. Not with so much as a feather, which is *pluma*, much less a *plancha*, which is flatiron.

So, I don't care *how* easy the guidebooks tell you it is to toss off a few fruity phrases in Flemish or Khasi or Plattdeutsch. The depressing truth is that any language simply bulges with laryngeal pitfalls and idiomatic ambushes.

The first time I went to Paris, I was 19—an age in which omniscience and obnoxiousness are mixed in equal portions. I spurned the provincialism of the typical tourist (the very word triggered sneers). I knew the deeper rewards that await a cultivated American who uses the patois of the natives. So I strode into a modest neighborhood bistro and hailed the *propriétaire* with a grand "Ah, M"sieur, but I am very hungry tonight!"

That, at least, is what I thought I was saying. What I actually uttered was, "Ah, but I shall have many a female tonight."

You can hardly blame the astounded *patron* for hustling me to a far and shadowy corner where my rampaging lust would cause no trouble. On the other hand, you can hardly blame me for having fallen victim to the treacherous nasalities of French, where the ever-so-slight difference in sound between *faim* and *femme* had converted a hungry adolescent into a sex maniac.

My greater downfall as a *manqué* Frenchman came about when I went to a railway station to inquire about trains to Nice. I came armed with a charming "Guide to Conversational French" I had picked up at a bargain (it was published in 1880) in a picturesque bookstall on the romantic Left Bank.

The charade between me and the cretin behind the bars took this form—to which I reserve all rights:

I (smiling): Bonjour, M'sieur! Is not this day reliable?

TICKET AGENT: You speak *French!* (he salutes): What joys! *Vive* the States United! May I wax your elbow?

I (modestly): *Voila!* To affairs?

TICKET AGENT (beaming): Advance.

I (chuckling): I demand you: When, dear Amy (*cher ami*), do gentleman trains go toward Lady Nice?

TICKETEER (enthusiastic): They are *very* nice chemises of iron, wet knight.

I (clearing throat): I fear I have been soft. What I intended to choke you is: "Pray recount such trains' *schedule!*"

TICKETEER (crying): Who can blame you? Do you ponder *I* perceive those swearing schedules? They are a sponge on French honor! They rife! They glut! They snore—

I: Please! What—*time*—does—the—train—

TICKETEER (slapping forehead): The *time?!* Smite my neck for buttering your confusion. It takes twelve hours from Paris.

I: No, no! I do not want the interval between farewelling Paris and helloing Nice. What I chattered was: "When —*when*—"

TICKETEER (excited): *Always* it occupies twelve hours! Saturdays, Sundays, apricots—bread pains—

I (moaning): Please, dear backache, speak *slower.*

TICKETEER: Slower, marches our *local* chemises! Naturally, the wagons are of diminished luxury—

I (shouting): Who denies: Merely recite! When shrink the trains from Paris to the south—*la Sud*—

TICKETEER (flinging hands heavenward): Ahh, a thousand apologies for my porcupine! Let us banish error once and for alright. Tray of beans: to reach the Sudan, you approximate Marseilles—

I: The *south*—

TICKEETER (puzzled): But the Sudan *is* south of dirty Marseilles!

I: —of *France!*

TICKETEER: It is south of France also! From Marseilles, you eat the bark off a boat—

I (hollering): Arrest! I do not gnaw vessels! I thirst but one dainty piece of entirely different *in-for-ma-tion!*

Fourteen hours later, I was in Innsbruck. Hold on: "Innsbruck" does begin with "in" and *is* a small piece of an entirely different nation.

*Alors,* then, my innocents, profit from my porcupine. Shun the natives' own locutions. Dodge the sly cedilla, the *accent grave,* the umbrageous umlaut. If you want to buy a drink in Budapest, just say: "Booze—on the rocks." To see a movie in Russia, hail a *muzhik:* "Sasha, which way to the RKO Lenin?"

If you're lost in Mozambique, stop any yokel with a bright "Blessings from your patron saint, and how do I get to the flea market?" Five will get you twenty if the peon doesn't take you by the hand and lead you there himself.

In the name of American mercy, why drive the locals *loco* by asking them to wallop yon horse with a parachute?

# 6

## THE ARTIST AND "REALITY":
### How We Are Taught to See

An artist is like other men—perhaps more sensitive, certainly more vulnerable. He is different in but one respect, and that one marks him a member of a special species: He has been endowed with that rare gift of the gods called talent. To some, like Fra Angelico, this was a blessing; to others, like Cézanne or Modigliani, it was a curse; but to every artist who ever lived—whether painter, poet, musician, or sculptor—his talent set him apart from his fellows.

The artist is driven by the demon of his talent—often beyond his capacity to understand, much less control. He is driven by the need to express that talent and, through it, to express himself. He is enslaved by the compulsion to share his feelings, his insight, his visions, his sense of revelation. Above all, he is beholden to the necessity of creating something (it may be beautiful, it may be horrifying) that did not exist before. He can create it only out of his own inner and insistent universe....

I never cease to marvel over the range of that beauty which

48

is captured on canvas or paper or wood, with pigments or pencil or chalks. Who cannot be impressed by the endless richness of art, the miraculous singularity of an artist's vision, the astounding variety of ways there are of seeing the world around us? Most of all, we must stand astonished before what painters have created out of their universe—to make it a new part of ours.

The simple but startling fact is this: painters *see* differently from the rest of us. This process we call "seeing," which we all take for granted, is unbelievably complicated. For we see not what is "there," but what *we have been taught to see there.*

The eye is a lens, to be sure, but that lens only receives images; and these images are referred back to the brain, where they must be patterned and given meaning. And meaning is a *convention* that stems from our training and our expectations. From the day we are born, our vision and our interpretations are molded to conform to prevailing modalities.... And then, some bold, original, immensely creative force breaks through the prevailing molds and makes us see anew. . . .

It is an astonishing fact that not until the thirteenth century did a Giotto break through the Byzantine tradition of painting figures full-length, seen directly head-on. He dared to paint *parts* of figures, half figures, figures cut off, or placed with their backs to the viewers—for the sake of something called composition.

It wasn't until the fifteenth century that it occurred to artists that you could look into, and not just at, a picture.

Rembrandt taught us that there is beauty in old people, in poor people, in apparently ugly faces.

Monet dared to paint what *he* saw, under varying conditions of light, and not what he was expected to see.

It wasn't until the end of the nineteenth century that artists had the nerve to do what children have always done—put color into shadows, paint metaphors, paint a green face because it is the face of envy, or a red face because it is the face of rage. Have we not chastised the freshness of children all these centuries by saying, "Now, Johnny, that's perfectly silly! That isn't the way a face (or an apple, or a tree) really looks!"

It wasn't until the late nineteenth century that artists exploited the discovery that warm colors seem to move toward the eye, that cool colors seem to recede, that the illusion of depth, on a two-dimensional surface, can be achieved through color itself! It was left for Cézanne to paint pictures which look as though they are coming toward us.

It was Degas, learning from the Japanese, who stubbornly insisted on capturing the unposed, the transient moment, and taught us to recognize the surpassing grace of the "ungraceful" —women bending, plopped on sofas, combing their hair, drying themselves.

It wasn't until Picasso and Braque that artists began to think of the possibility of revealing several, or all, sides of an object in an effort to show us a larger-than-front-focus view.

Has it not dawned on you that none of us can *see* any longer the way our ancestors did? We no longer can see as men saw before the modern artists. You can't see a bowl of fruit the way it was seen before Cézanne. You can't see a cathedral without having been altered by Monet. You can't see fish in an aquarium without having been influenced by Klee.

We see not what is real (a phantom, after all, is "real" enough to the person terrified by it), but what we have been conditioned to think of as being real. What we call reality is not much more than the perceptions we allow to pass through the filters of our conditioning.

We all live, in part, within the conceptual prison of the past.

The central point was stated by Constable, who said that seeing is itself an art, and that even seeing nature is an art that must be learned. Degas, that irascible genius, declared: "Drawing is not what one sees, but what others have to be made to see."

Does this idea seem preposterous? The brilliant art authority E. H. Gombrich reminds us that ancient artists used to draw

eyelashes on the lower lids of horses. There are no lashes on
the lower eyelids of horses. Still, the artists "saw" them there—
because they were so accustomed to seeing lashes on men's
lower lids. Leonardo da Vinci, as skillful a recorder of "reality"
as you could ask for, made certain mistakes in drawing the heart,
from cadavers opened for examination, because he had been
reading Galen—and Galen was wrong. Even so impeccable a
draftsman as Dürer made certain errors in drawing the human
eye because his own vision was skewed by the fallacious stereo-
types of his day.

Chinese artists were instructed to record not what they "see"—
but what they feel about what they see. They use a brush as
Western poets use words—to express emotions, not record literal
images. When the Impressionists began to use color to express
feelings, when they put the green of envy or the red of anger
into the human face, or color into shadows, they shocked eyes
that had, since the Renaissance, been taught to see a different
constellation of visibilities.

So reality changes for us as we free ourselves from the crippling
restrictions of the preconceived. "We see things as *we* are, not as
*they* are." It is the great, revolutionary role of the artist to liberate
us from the prisons of the familiar.

Does all this seem unreal to you? Do you believe in a real-
ness, an absoluteness of things which are visible to anyone and
everyone alike? Perhaps you do. Perhaps you are thinking,
"All this is intellectual quibbling. Reality is simple enough.
Just set a camera down and press the trigger—and *that* will
record exactly what is 'there!'"

Well, let us test that out. Suppose you take a camera and
set out to photograph, say, a house. Any house. You want "just
a picture of a house." Now consider the decisions you will
have to make—consciously or unconsciously, intuitively or by
default. From what distance shall the house be photographed?
From far away? From near? From the "middle"? Then at what

angle? How high? How low? All these depend, of course, on what kind of picture you want—indeed, what kind of house you want to portray. And that depends on what impression or mood or atmosphere or detail you want to present. If the house is seen from a low angle, that will emphasize its height. If seen from a hill looking down, it will look different. "Just straight on," you say? Very well. Is the sycamore to the left to be included? The azalea on the right? The ridge beyond? Will you include the rail fence there, the rock here, the curving path? You will soon notice that each position, each view changes the total field of vision—and each contains its own cluster of characteristics.

Don't get impatient; this is but the beginning. Consider the light now. Shall it come from the left, the right, overhead, from behind? And how much light do you want? You can choose the time of day in which to shoot; you can use reflectors to diminish shadows, or floodlights, flashbulbs to light up what is dark or highlight a feature you want to stress. You can also manipulate light by varying the opening of your lens; you can even create an illusion of dawn or dusk. And by changing the opening of your lens, you create new *contexts,* because groups of details can be made to come into focus, or be thrown out of it.

"Enough!" you cry? But you have much more to decide. Do you want to make this house crisp-clear in all its details—shutters, windows, shingles? That will also make sharp a mass of unpretty and distracting objects around. Do you want the scene made pastoral, scary, sad? Shall the sky be ignored or brought forward? A filter can make the clouds leap toward the eye. Even moonlight need not be the prerogative of the moon alone; infrared film can transform the sun into its sister.

And by the way, what kind of film will you use? "Just black and white!" you protest? Ah, but there is no such thing as "just black and white." Different films give different effects, different modulations of light and shade, different hues of gray, different textures and grains.

Well, suppose you take your picture, whatever it is. You are in the darkroom now. You have your negative. You are about to print your picture. And now a new army of possibilities marches before you. You can print any *part* of the picture. You can "crop" out the top, the bottom, either side or both. You can magnify a detail to achieve a quite unexpected effect. You can darken or lighten the overall light. You can even manipulate the very lines and planes, to get calculated distortions, by tilting your paper. You can convert the projection lens into a sort of microscope or telescope. You can soften your original focus. You can take that innocuous house you recorded on film and endow it with shadows or highlights, make it saccharine or sinister. You can change the visual impact by selecting different papers on which to print your image. You can—but perhaps this is enough.

Now everything I have said about photographing a house is, of course, equally (or more) true of photographing a face or a flower, a landscape or a still life; recording a skyline, a boy biting into a hot dog, a girl blowing on a trumpet; trying to capture raindrops on a rose, or gulls in the air, or ants on a blade of grass.

No two photographers take precisely the same picture of the identical subject—even if they try to, because there are different emotions and mentalities behind the different lenses. The difference between a photograph taken by an amateur and one taken by a master is as great as the difference between a jingle and a sonata.

If what I have said here is true of photography, consider now how much more powerfully it applies to painting. Any camera, lens, film, or filter contains certain mechanical limitations—none of which confines the painter. An artist can draw what no camera can photograph. No camera can record the images in a man's mind. No camera contains the flexibility and resourcefulness of the human hand, to say nothing of the immense imaginative possibilities of the human brain.

It is the multitudinous differences—in vision and visual sensitivity; in the sensing of arrangement and accident; in the apprehension of line, light, color, form, mass, space; in recognizing unsuspected attributes of beauty, power, grace; in opening new windows of perception to surprise—it is the wonderful variations in these, to say nothing of differences in sheer skill, which distinguish the creative artist from his fellow men.

As Leonardo put it: "If the painter wishes to see beauties to fall in love with, it is in his power to bring them forth, and if he wants to see monstrous things that frighten or are foolish or laughable or indeed to be pitied, he is their Lord and God."

The artist, I have said, frees us from the bonds of tradition. He gives us new eyes, eyes with which we can see "reality" anew and, more importantly, with which we can see aspects of reality we did not dream were there. They were not, in fact, there—until he created them out of his vision, his active transformation of reality, his creating something to be seen for the first time. A Japanese master was once asked, "What is the most difficult part of a picture?" He answered, "The part that is to be left out."

My use of the word "artist," I should note, is not limited to painters. Poets, scientists, novelists; musicians, sculptors, essayists; dancers, philosophers, architects—each provided mankind with images and visions and insights that totally transformed the world with whose prevailing perceptions they had been indoctrinated.

A Shakespeare or T. S. Eliot or Robert Frost opens new doors to our experience of the "real world." A Mozart or Mahler, Beethoven or Bartók created aural adventures unknown before. Copernicus or Einstein revolutionized our imaginings of the universe about which our ancestors have wondered since the days of the cave. A Praxiteles or Michelangelo, Henry Moore or Alexander Calder, radically altered our aesthetic awareness of form. And who can gauge the magnitude of the inner world Dostoevsky or Freud lifted out of the preceding darkness? And who would deny the new dimensions of movement and design which grew from the genius of a Pavlowa, a Fokine, Balanchine? I focus attention on painters because their art *seems* so closely

related to the ordinary things we see every day, and because each
of us in our infancy played with the joyous ingredients of drawing and color. There is no scientific parallel to a pencil, no
musical equivalent of a crayon, no philosophical antecedent
(save wonder) of play with beads and sand.

My point about art and artists simply can be made more vivid
and visible than the same point about Heraclitus, say, or Archi-
medes or Euclid, Lobachevsky or Reimann or Fred Hoyle. Those
aspects of my thesis are touched upon in a later chapter.

We have all been taught, through the eyes and minds of
artists, to extract meaning from the confusing, unstructured
plentitude of objects, details, impressions, distractions that clamor
all around us.

We have all been led to find beauty where previous generations did not dream it lay concealed—or uncreated. There is
truth, no less than mischief, in Oscar Wilde's aphorism: "Nature
imitates art."

The moral to all this is perhaps best found, as it so often is,
in an anecdote. A woman who "knew what she liked in art" was
visiting Matisse's studio. She studied the painting on his easel
for a while, then said, "You have made the arm on that girl
much too *long*."

"Madame," said Matisse, "that is not a girl; it is a picture."

# 7

---

## DELICIOUS SCOUNDRELS

**I** once published a little item about a genius (name unknown) who placed the following advertisement in the ever-so-sober Personals column of the ever-so-lucrative Los Angeles *Times:*

LAST DAY TO SEND IN YOUR DOLLAR!
—BOX 124

That's all the ad said.

Thousands of simpletons, osteocephalics, and run-of-the-mill *schlemiels* fell all over themselves getting their dollars into Box 124 "in time." In time for what? For the last day to send in their dollar. Go argue with Human Nature.

Well, my paragraph drew such a flurry of mail from avaricious readers that I had to warn them not to try to publish such an ad themselves—because the federal authorities had cracked down on the anonymous genius of Box 124, making him aware of the consequences that might follow such a brazen, shameless, ingenious advertisement. It constituted some sort of fraud via the U.S. mails—than which no fraud can be fraudier, or fraughtier with risk.

My legal consultant tells me that the law has never been able to devise all-inclusive statutes about larceny, which embraces such subtleties of dupery as the old shell game, the beaver dodge, the perennial sale of "mink" or "sable" freshly "stolen" from tony fur salons, or the transfer of toll rights to the Verrazzano Bridge.

But there just is no doubt that if you go around promising future felicities with excessive imagination, or describing imaginary bonanzas with undue persuasiveness, or agreeing to grow hair on bald pates, or restore passion to depleted gonads—and if you actually advertise such demonstrations of faith in P. T. Barnum's Law (anent the minute-by-minute production of suckers), do not be surprised if a bailiff knocks on your door.

I have often pondered the curious fondness we all feel (in greater or lesser degrees of self-candor) for those colorful scoundrels in our midst who pit their wits against probity. Our personal rectitude (which is learned) may condemn swindlers and boodlers for their trickery, but our delight in hanky-panky (which is native) secretly dotes on their ingenuity. In their daydreams even judges must sigh with *subpoena* envy.

W. C. Fields, the most withering con man Hollywood ever allowed to go unpunished (according to the old Hays Code), once leered, "You can't cheat an honest man." That moralism has practically become the Eleventh Commandment in American folk thought: It *is* a noble idea, but it is not true.

Consider, for instance, the many victims of an uncaught *maestro* of skulduggery in Watchung, New Jersey. One Saturday night, just before Labor Day, this scoundrel placed a night-deposit box outside the entrance to a branch bank in a large shopping center on Route 22. He set his beautifully made night-deposit box, which was a fake, right next to the bank's night-deposit box, which was authentic. Since banks are closed on Sundays and Labor Day, one of the busiest weekends of the year, it is scarcely surprising that storekeepers were tickled pink to deposit their cash, and checks made out to "cash," into the night-depository boxes.

Early Tuesday morning the monetary wizard who had placed

the fake night-deposit receptacle next to the bank's real one quickly reclaimed his brain child. The illicit gain to our dastardly deceiver came to over $26,000 in cash, $3,500 in checks, and who knows how much exultation and professional pride?

The police force of Watchung, New Jersey, refused to tell the Associated Press exactly what the fake depository box looked like. This was quite correct of them, in my opinion.

Excessive verisimilitude in reporting criminal artifacts is pretty certain to: (a) instruct and (b) encourage maleficent imitators. Only a fool would publicly provide a good working description of a fake bank night-deposit box.

I even worry whether my recounting of this whole shameful episode may not spur a rash of false boxes or post-office windows in, say, Greenwich, Connecticut, which offers considerably more lucrative opportunities for the exploitation of confidence than did the modest shopping center on Route 22.

As for the name Watchung, I marvel at the esthetic satisfaction that nomenclature can provide.

W. C. Fields was not *entirely* wrong, of course. One of my favorite childhood memories involves a men's clothing store in our neighborhood, which was owned by a pair of partners who, rumor had it, sent eight children through college simply by pretending to be deaf. The ingenious haberdashers' deaf caper is unmatched, I think, for simplicity, duplicity, and punishment to the greedy. Here is how it worked:

One partner would wait on a customer, extolling the excellence of the wool, the styling, the needlework of this or that suit. Often the customer would, naturally, ask, "How much is this suit?"

"What?" asked the salesman, cupping his ear.

"How—much—does—it—cost?" the customer repeated more loudly.

"Hanh?"

"*How much is the suit?*" the customer would shout.

"Ah, the *price!* I'll ask the boss." Whereupon the "clerk" would turn and shout toward the back of the store: "*How much is the beautiful navy-blue, double-breasted suit?*"

The "boss" would shout back: "*Forty dollars!*"

The "deaf" clerk would tell the customer: "The boss says, 'Twenty dollars.'"

Need I describe how swiftly many otherwise righteous men, young and old, plunked down their twenty dollars and hastened out of the store, chortling? Scoundrels at heart, they deserved W. C. Fields' scorn.

Which brings me to a third type of fraudulence: the harmless practical joke—not because it is a joke but because it sometimes executes Justice.

A classmate of mine at college (let's call him Theobald Prysock) grew so disgusted by the silly hazings he had to endure as a freshman "pledge" to a certain fraternity that he decided to quit. But moral outrage so burned within the soul of Theobald Prysock that he could not simply return his pledge pin. He hungered for the *geste juste,* the perfect touch of Tisiphone (look him up yourself).

Well, Theobald spent days on end seeking an act of reprisal that would properly express his feelings for the fraternity "brothers" he was disowning. What he finally did was masterful:

One night, after his peers were all snoring away, Theobald tiptoed down the stairs of the fraternity house to the fraternity library. He closed the door, removed a book, turned to the flyleaf, and inscribed therein:

GIFT

OF

THEOBALD PRYSOCK

He put the book back on the shelf and proceeded to the next....

It took my pal Theobald a good four hours, I believe, to donate the entire library of Phi Gimmel Epsilon—to itself.

Can you imagine a happier soul than Theo, his lavish, costless philanthropy completed, as he carried his suitcase into the night?

I feel privileged to have known such a rogue.

# 8

## YOU GOTTA HAVE FAITH—IN REASON

I always marvel over the miracle of Reasoning (it deserves a capital), when demonstrated by one of my fellow-members of the most advanced of primates. I chortle even more when I encounter a feat of analytic clarity performed by someone who would be classed as "uneducated," in any poll—someone totally untutored, unsophisticated, bereft of the slightest familiarity with the formal laws of logic or methodology.

I have just come across something that fortifies my faith in the capacity of men to think lucidly (a faith not easy to maintain in these lunar times)—a statement by an eighteenth century Seneca Indian named Handsome Lake. He had gone to no school, no Day Camp, no Play Group. He had received no federal aid from Operation Head Start, Store Front, or Remedial Reading. In fact, he could not read at all. He had not even received a Fulbright to broaden his mind abroad.

Handsome Lake was a true child of nature, and so stout a believer in the dangers of alcohol (at least to Indians) that he went around urging temperance upon his tribesmen. To prove his point and drive home his message, Handsome Lake put his argument in this form:

> Some say there is no harm in fermented liquids. Then let this plan be tried: let your men gather in two parties, one consuming a feast of apples and corn, the other a feast of cider and whiskey. Let the parties be evenly divided and evenly matched. Let them commence feasting at the same time.... Now, when the feasting is finished, you will see those who drank the intoxicating juices murder one of their own party; but not so those who ate only the apples and corn.

I ask you: where is there a better, cleaner example of reason, scientific method, or the controlled experiment?*

So when anyone starts questioning the transcendent power of native (no pun) intelligence, whether measured by I.Q. or any other tested test; or when someone mistakes schooling for education, or when someone peddles clap-trap about the "fatal" effects of a disadvantaged neighborhood—just quote Handsome Lake. And bow your head in homage.

*Note to racists, non-racists, Jensenists, anti-Jensenites, geneticists, environmentalists, and Aunt Agatha:*

I do *not* mean to suggest that the shining example of Handsome Lake proves that Indians are brighter than Indianians; or that I.Q. tests are irrelevant; or that I.Q. tests are decisive; or that any test tests *all* types of ability; or that all the members of one or another race are intrinsically more intelligent (or less intelligent) than *all* the members of another race.

I will go even further: Some Arabs are smarter than some

---

* Since you will be clamoring to know where I ran across this exquisite passage, I am happy to tell you: I don't remember. What my notes do tell me, though, is that Handsome Lake was quoted by one A. C. Parker, in a *New York State Museum Bulletin No. 163* (1913). I would frame it in gold, if I had a copy.

Jews, many Negroes are smarter than many whites—but vice versa.

What is foolishly ignored in the passionate disputations about Inheritance and Environment is the obvious fact that our I.Q. tests do not measure human skills/potential in a hundred admirable fields: composing music, making sauces, lifting weights, fording streams, raising orchids, creating ballets, tying Christmas packages, painting portraits, performing card tricks, singing hymns, propelling kayaks, laying mosaics, playing the harmonica, swimming the back stroke, fitting watch-parts, dreaming in color, mixing cement, mending china, writing poems, breeding butterflies, tarring roofs, etc. I.Q. tests are not even an infallible measure of skill in constructing I.Q. tests. *That* cuts to the bone. Has anyone checked the intelligence of people who devise intelligence tests?

Let me remind you that there is no Allah but Allah, and Mohammed (who never took a Stanford-Binet or any other test) was certainly his Prophet.

Let us proceed with plaudits to another man who exercised the precious powers of reason.

In a certain pleasant town, where I spend my summers, a Mr. and Mrs. Goodfellow live in a pleasant house right next to Mr. and Mrs. Lout (the names are made up, to protect the idiots). Mr. and Mrs. Goodfellow are pleasant, law-abiding folk, who tend their own pleasant lawn, mind their own pleasant business, and give offense to neither man nor beast nor fowl. Mr. and Mrs. Lout, on the other hand, are unpleasant boors, who keep their television sets turned up full volume, periodically throw cups and saucers at each other in domestic squabbles, and specialize in all-night brawls with a gang of boozy, raucous friends.

Many has been the time Mr. or Mrs. Goodfellow politely and pleasantly requested Mr. or Mrs. Lout to *please* turn down the T.V., or de-decibelize their domestic spats, or kindly tell their moronic guests to quiet down so that bodies up and down the street might get a decent night's sleep. And on each occasion, the Louts replied by telling the Goodfellows to get lost, drop dead, or go to Hell. The excruciating brayings and brawlings and blatterings from the Lout's domicile proceeded undiminished —to wreck the peaceful, pacific life of the Goodfellows.

Now what would you do with neighbors like that? Inform the cops? Well, people in our pleasant summer town are allowed to "enjoy themselves" until, say, midnight—and the Louts and their repulsive guests were the type who pay no mind whatsoever to warnings from the *polizei* which are not reinforced by either punitive muscle or a forcible trip to the local clink—neither of which has transpired.

Would you beat up Mr. Lout? Alas, Mr. Goodfellow is a *nebbish*, a teacher of literature, whereas Mr. Lout is a 16½"-neck-size bruiser who runs a trucking firm after a blood-thirsty career as a professional wrestler. To make the contrast more dramatic I should tell you that whereas Mr. Goodfellow's nickname is "Lolly," Mr. Lout's nickname is "Spike."

So what can a Lolly do vis-à-vis a Spike? Well what Mr. Goodfellow did do ranks, in my mind, with the shrewdest feats of *quid pro quo* in the history of human justice.

Lolly placed a tape recorder out on his porch one summer night, and recorded the ear-shattering caperings of the party going on full swing on the porch of his unpleasant neighbor.... And the next morning, when the accumulated beer and Bourbon bottles had not even been swept off the porch stairs by the drunken, hung-over Louts, Goodfellow put the tape on his hi-fi set, turned it on full blast, pointed the two speakers out of the open windows right toward Spike's bedroom, and went for a trip to the beach with his wife. All day long, the sounds of the Lout's savagery assailed the ears of the perpetrators....

The peace and quiet that characterized the subsequent behavior of the Louts and their vulgar guests is beyond my powers of gloating. Never was retribution doled out in such exact, equitable measure.

Reason, my friends, *can* prevail.

# 9

## BERTRAND RUSSELL AND GOD

Whenever I run across Bertrand Russell's name, I remember several afternoons I spent with him in London, years ago, in his home on Queen's Road.

He was very thin, frail, and skin-creased, shorter than I had assumed, with a head much too large for his body, a bright-eyed elf with an aureole of white hair and a thread of a mouth that twisted—sardonic or amused, petulant or defiant—with every turn of his mood.

A pipe was never out of his hands. Whenever I asked him a question, he would fuss and fiddle with that pipe, tamping it down or reaming it, blowing into its stem to clean the passage, filling it, lighting it slowly, tapping it out or refilling it—and then his answer would emerge, pellucid in phrasing and breathtaking in precision Never have I encountered such a flow of epigrams, or such tantalizing fugues of intelligence and irony. He used his pipe as a prop—to give him time to think, formulating his response, editing it, polishing it, rehearsing it, I suspect, before he presented it to me. The result was intoxicating.

He was cool in manner, I should say—perhaps because he was suspicious of my purpose: I had written to say I hoped to persuade him to write a 5,000-word article on agnosticism (for *Look* magazine). Almost his first words were: "I very much doubt that your editor will publish—in America—what I should want to say."

(One must remember how shabbily Russell had been treated by the city of New York, judged "unfit" to teach at City College, and fired, despite his contract, becauses of his "lecherous, lustful, erotomaniac, aphrodisiac ... writings," the complaint read.)

He asked, "What sort of article have you in mind?"

"A question-answer format ..."

"And who," he murmured, "will put the questions?"

"I."

Pause. Puff. Smoke. "Do give me some examples."

"Are you an agnostic or an atheist?" I asked.

"Agnostic, of course.... Atheists are like Christians: that is, both maintain that we can know whether or not there is a God. The Christian holds that we *can* know God exists; the atheist holds that we know that God does not. But the agnostic knows that we do not know enough, that we do not possess sufficient grounds, either to affirm *or* deny the existence of a supreme being.... So I believe that although the existence of God is not impossible, it is improbable. Quite improbable."

"How do you explain the beauty and harmony of nature?"

He cocked his head to one side like a mischievous sparrow: "I fail to see much beauty or harmony in a tapeworm.... Animals throughout the kingdom of 'beautiful' nature, kill and prey upon each other, quite without mercy. The stars in the 'harmonious' heavens explode from time to time, and destroy everything in their vicinity. Beauty is entirely subjective. It can exist only in the eye—and the mind—of an observer.... Try another question."

"Well, do you ever—however vaguely or infrequently—fear God, or God's judgment?"

Russell shrugged. "*If* there is, in fact, a Supreme Deity, which

I doubt, I think it most unlikely that he—" a pause, an ironic grimace—"would possess so uneasy a vanity as to be offended by my views about his existence." He fixed me with a skeptical stare. "Now then, will your magazine print such scandalous comments for the God-fearing American public?" His lips corkscrewed both dubiety and disdain.

"I can assure you that we will."

"Perhaps you had better ask more questions."

"Do you deny that man has a soul?" I asked.

A moue traversed his lips. "What do you mean by 'soul'? One can't give a precise answer to an imprecise question."

"I suspect, sir, that you know what men mean when they talk about the soul."

"Mmh," he shrugged. "I suppose that 'soul' is meant to designate some non-material essence, temporarily associated with man's corporeal existence—an essence, in the case of those who believe in immortality, that presumably leaves man's body to continue its existence, in one form or another, throughout all of the future....I do not believe any of this, of course." He blinked. "But that should in no way lead you to think I am a materialist. I am just as doubtful about the reality of the body...."

"Then do you in any way distinguish between mind and matter?"

"That," he sighed, "takes us into rather difficult problems in metaphysics. For my part, 'mind' and 'matter' are merely symbols, conveniences used in philosophical discourse."

"Don't you think that matter exists?"

"There are powerful reasons for holding that neither mind nor matter exist."

"That, I suppose, would lead you to deny that there is a hereafter."

A cloud of smoke appeared from his pipe. "I have failed to find any persuasive evidence, even—" (dryly) "—in the earnest allegations of spiritualists, transmigrationists, or physical researchers, that leads me to take seriously the assumption that we, or parts of us, survive death. But I remain open to the conviction; if respectable data ever come along, I should examine them with maximum care." The tone suggested that Russell was confident such data were not likely to consume much of his time in the years ahead. "You know, agnosticism simply baffles many people.... When I was sent to prison as a pacifist, during the First World War, the warder, after asking the conventional questions—name, birth-date, place of residence—asked what was my religion. 'I am an agnostic,' I said. The poor man—a very decent sort—looked bewildered. 'A what?' he asked. 'Agnostic,' I repeated. He said, '*Would* you be so good as to spell that out?' So I spelled out 'a—g—n' and so on. When the warder read the strange word he had written, he looked up cheerfully and said, 'Well, there certainly are a great many religious sects—but I am sure they all worship the same God!'" Russell smiled; he would not, I think, elevate his amusement with a laugh.

"What about so-called miracles?" I asked. "Miraculous cures, for example?"

Russell waved a hand in benign dismissal of divine therapy. "My dear boy, faith certainly does heal—some people. But that scarcely proves anything 'miraculous.' Even at Lourdes, some diseases and afflictions and physical disabilities have never been cured.... Those pious people who experience a cure at Lourdes could probably have been cured in another place, or by some physician, if they possessed the same certainty of faith."

"What about the miracles in the Bible?"

An expression of pain (or dismay) preceded the answer: "Even learned churchmen, if enlightened, think of the Bible as do I: Not as holy revelation, but as a compilation of early history, folk-tales, myths—no more exact than, say, the *Iliad* or the *Odyssey*.... All known religions contain an ample supply of lofty legends, and 'revelations' about phenomena which the knowledge of their time—and their sages—could not explain. ...I daresay that Homer makes as good a case for the gods of Greece as Moses made for the God of Israel."

After his young wife brought us tea, I asked, "What is the meaning of life to an agnostic?"

"What is the meaning of 'the meaning of life'?" he retorted.

"I do not believe that life has meaning; it just happens. Individual men and women have their own goals and purposes; and nothing in agnosticism need cause them to surrender those goals or alter those purposes."

"Are many agnostics Communists? Do they not both oppose religion?"

"Not at all. Communism simply opposes religions other than itself. Marxism is a set of virulent and intolerant dogmas. Agnostics must therefore oppose it with all their powers."

I asked, "Let us suppose, sir, that after you have left this sorry vale, you actually found yourself in heaven, standing before the Throne. There, in all His glory, sat the Lord—not Lord Russell, sir: God." Russell winced. "What would you think?"

"I would think I was dreaming."

"But suppose you realized you were not? Suppose that there, before your eyes, beyond a shadow of a doubt, *was* God. What would you say?"

The pixie wrinkled his nose. "I probably would ask, 'But sir, why did you not give me better evidence?'"

There is a noteworthy end to my story. After *Look* printed Russell's colloquy, the New York *Daily News* ran a blistering editorial to the effect that Bertrand Russell's shocking ruminations proved that there *must* be a merciful God: how else could one explain "the continued existence" of so unpleasant, wicked, and muddle-headed a philosopher?

I sent Russell the editorial. His reply (which I publish by permission of his estate) is vintage irony:

DEAR MR. ROSTEN:

Thank you for sending me the extract from the N.Y. "Daily News."

I think the evidence for the existence of God supplied by my continued existence is strengthened by the continued existence of the N.Y. "Daily News." It and I can agree in wishing that His mercy were less infinite.

Yours sincerely,
BERTRAND RUSSELL

To my surprise, the "His" was capitalized. All else illustrates Russell's unique combination of reasoning and mockery.

I sometimes think the great agnostic could have invented the epigram whose author no one knows: "Let us thank God that there is no God."

Russell certainly would have liked the story of the atheist and the priest, who asked him, "But how can you be so very positive that God does not exist?"

The atheist huffed, "Well, a man has to believe in *some*thing!"

# 10

---

## EPISODE NEAR MUNICH

**T**he things that are hardest to bear are sweetest to remember," wrote Seneca. What nonsense. How kindly memory represses the anguished moments of the past. Life would be unbearable were we unable to forget.

The other night, some friends were talking about the War (I mean the Big War, called II), and suddenly, with the sharpness of a knife thrust, I remembered something pushed into the cellars of my mind long ago. It is not easy for me to write about it.

It was 1945, just after the Nazis collapsed. I was on a special mission out of Paris, for what was soon to become SHAEF, meaning "Supreme Headquarters American Expeditionary Forces in Europe." (The commander of SHAEF was Dwight D. Eisenhower.)

We were driving from Augsburg to Munich—"Tex," my GI driver; Major O'Neill; and I, a civilian in officer's uniform, with the lofty rank of colonel ("assimilated").

It had been raining for two days—a harsh, very cold rain. We swept around a wide curve in the road, and I saw a figure far ahead, marching toward us, head down, shoulders hunched. It wore no hat, no coat. As we came closer, I saw it was a young man. He was soaking wet. The rain dripped off his hair. His shirt stuck to his wet skin. A rucksack was half-slung across his back.

I had seen hundreds of people plodding down the roads of France and Germany this way: alone, in groups, silent, beaten, stunned. But there was a curious jauntiness in this boy's pace that caught my attention.

I told Tex to stop.

The boy on the road slowed down warily, but when he spotted the U.S. Army star on our car, his face lit up. "Hollo, *Amerikaner!*"

"Hello. *Wie weit ist München?*" I asked.

"*München? Ja.* Oh—thirty kilometers, sir." He spoke in Yiddish. "*Aber,* I am no German! No, no! Look." He was jabbing at a red cloth triangle sewed onto his shirt: it was the badge Jews had been forced to wear. He rolled up a wet sleeve, and I saw the sign of a concentration abbatoir: numbers tattooed on his forearm in blue.

"Get in," I told the boy.

He clambered in next to Tex.

"Which camp were you in?" I asked.

"Dachau."

"Where are you going?"

He pointed to the west.

"*Where?*"

He shrugged. "To France, maybe. Holland. Anywhere. Then, I hope, America. Everyone wants to go to America. I have a relative there! An aunt. My mother's sister. I never saw her, you understand, because she left Poland before I was born, but my mother got letters from her before the war....I would like to get word to my aunt. About me. Being alive, I mean. She's the only member of our family still alive. I just want her to know. That's all. If someone was glad I survived—well, that would make a difference."

"What's he saying?" O'Neill asked me.

I told him.

He fumbled for a cigarette. O'Neill was the toughest-looking Irishman you ever saw, and he wore a shoulder holster with a fearful .45 bulging in it. The pistol had given me great comfort until I learned that "Buzz," a PR joker, was afraid to load it. ("Scares hell out of you *un*loaded, right?" He certainly was right.)

"Your aunt," I said to the boy. "What's her name?"

"I don't know. She married."

"Do you know her address?"

"Her address." The boy sighed. "That's the trouble. I don't remember. I had her whole name and address in a little notebook. But when they took us into Dachau they lined us all up in the snow and told us to undress—naked, absolutely naked. I had that little notebook in my pocket, with my aunt's name and address in it, and I took the notebook out of my pocket as I took all my clothes off, but one of the Nazi guards grabbed the book out of my hands and threw it on the pile of other things. I asked him if he wouldn't please let me keep just one page. He hit me with his gun and knocked me down. Then all the men were herded into a room—and there they tattooed numbers on our arms."

"What's he saying?" O'Neill asked.

I told him.

"Oh, Jesus."

"I never really knew my *uncle's* name," the boy said. "I just figured it was in the notebook. ... And the address—how many times, in the camp, I tried to remember it! But all I could bring back was that it was in New York, and the street was a number, and it had four numbers. Every night, before I'd fall asleep, I tried to bring that address back to my mind. ... All I want is for my aunt to know. It's nice to think one person in the world is glad I got out alive. ..."

"Isn't there any part of the address you remember?"

He frowned. "I think the numbers began One Eight. ... That's all I remember."

I did not know what to say. I asked, "Did you report this to the Americans?"

"Oh, yes. The Displaced Persons authorities, the Red Cross—they were all nice. They filled out forms.... But what could they do? What can anyone do?"

We gave him a poncho, some soap, chocolate, K rations, and cigarettes. The boy made a halfhearted gesture of refusal, but O'Neill told him not to be a damned fool.

The boy stuffed the things into his rucksack. "The cigarettes are very valuable," he said. "I can trade them." He slipped the poncho over his head and burst into a grin. "This is *won*derful!"

I wrote my name and APO number on a slip of paper. "Look, if you ever do remember any more—about your aunt or uncle's address—write me. Or ask one of our soldiers. They'll do it."

"If I could only remember," he said.

He got out of the car and started down the road to the west. Once he turned to wave to us, and I saw that he was wolfing the chocolate.

"Goddamn it, Parks!" O'Neill suddenly shouted at Tex. "What the hell you waiting for? Get the lead out of your ass! Move it! *Move!*"

Soon we splashed through some miserable village, and O'Neill stuck his head out of the window and kept yelling, "*Schwein!* Sonsabitches! Dirty, rotten murderers! Murderers, *mur-der-ers!*"

In Munich we got drunk quite quickly. All Buzz O'Neill did was curse and shout obscenities I can hear even now.

# 11

## CREATIVITY AND SCIENCE

The history of man's politics is a shameful chronicle of violence, vanity and vengeance—laced with endless greed, inflated ambitions and parochial fears.

The history of man's beliefs is an absurd story of ignorance, credulity, superstition, infantile terror and magical beguilements.

The history of man's ideas is a story of incredible stupidity, relieved by the occasional, sparkling eruption of original minds.

All through the history of our sad human race, intelligence has been besieged by ignorance, inquiry has been harassed by fanaticism, ideas have been strangled by dogmas.

It is impossible to spend twenty-four hours on this planet without encountering several hundred examples of folly, irrationality, lunacy, self-deception, outrageous buncombe, or rank idolatry. Common sense is certainly not very common. Reason is rare in human affairs. *Non sequiturs* seem to be dear to the human heart. Preference or wish-fulfillment seems to enlist the most powerful and passionate legions of mankind.

I sometimes think that the central fact about our race—the

one commanding generalization—is this: We see things as *we* are, not as they are. I said this before; let me expand it.

All of our perceptions are partial, crippled recognitions of the realities around us. We see what we want to see and hear what we want to hear, and we are terrified by the need to restructure our intellectual universe. We feel threatened by truly new ideas. We see things as we are—like the lady at the cocktail party who said to her husband, "Dear, don't you think you had better stop drinking—your face is already beginning to get blurred."

The power of habit is so great, the path of acceptance so safe, that the alteration of conventions is always slow and painful. That is why the creative mind, the creative thinker, the creative observer is crucially important in human history. Notice I do not say "the intellectual": for many extremely creative people are not intellectuals. Many intellectuals are not too intelligent; and very few intellectuals are creative. The one thing that the intellectual can contribute is resolute poise in the presence of new and threatening ideas.

The ideas of Newton, which baffled all but a handful of men in his time, are quite easily understood by high-school students today. The ideas of Einstein, which you and I find so difficult to comprehend, will not be very difficult for the next generation. Such concepts as the curvature of space, or relativity, or indeterminism, or infinity itself, become less difficult to comprehend as time passes, because those who learn them afresh do not have to break through the prison of what they already have been taught. They have escaped the crippling effects of education.

There is a special irony in what I am saying. Not so long ago, in these United States, the target of political disdain and contempt was that pathetic, unrealistic, useless person—"the egghead." You may remember that a former Secretary of Defense turned down a project for basic research with this comment: "Basic research is when you don't know what it is you're trying to find out."

Now, aside from the appalling syntax, which suggests that the Secretary had not taken the trouble to learn how to construct a sentence in his native tongue, the position he expounded is absurd: for if there is anything that research, or thought, or exploration is *incapable* of being, it is "useless." In one sense, no experiment ever fails: it tells us that some factors do not necessarily correlate. Thomas Edison, being consoled after 8,000 unsuccessful attempts to make a nickel-iron storage battery, cheerfully remarked, "But we now know eight thousand things that won't work!"

The most practical things in this world are not dynamos, nor computers, nor aircraft; the most practical things are *ideas*. It is from some curious, abstract, "impractical egghead" that our most marvelous gadgets come.

The contempt of practical men for curious men, or of "realists" for "just theoreticians," rests on nothing more than ignorance—plus egotism.

Now the free man, the curious man, will always disturb his society, because he confronts freshly what is conventional. He dares to reexamine what seems to others to be "obvious." The writer, the thinker, the artist, the scientist, have this in common: they are engaged in a life-long struggle to free themselves from the familiar.

Every day in the United States, in some home with a child of, say, seven, a parent is asked the question, "Why is two and two four?" And every day the answer is given, "Now, Johnny, don't be silly. It just *is*." In fact, the question is extremely interesting and elegant, to which many answers can be given—not the least important of which is that two and two make four in but *one* system of counting; we might devise others in which four is not necessarily right.

Every day in the United States, children are brought right up to a moment of great importance in human experience, but are not told how exciting and fruitful this moment can be. The moment comes during drills about the multiplication table. "Johnny, how much is two and two?"

"Four."

"Mary, how much is two times three?"

"Six."

"Jack, two times *what* equals ten?"

Jack says "Five," and the lesson proceeds; and the great, germinal moment is passed. For the teacher or parent *could* have said, "At this moment you are standing before one of the great inventions of the human mind—the concept of X. 'Two times *what* equals ten?' can also be put this way, 'Two X equal ten.' "

That miraculous X, the unknown, can be taught at a very early age, with excitement, and not deferred until our less-sharpened sensibilities are introduced to that astonishing, unpopular subject called algebra.

Over and over, it is our fallacy to teach a convention as if it is an irrevocable truth. As parents, as teachers, as citizens, we go on teaching one way of thinking as if it is *the* way of thinking. We all cling to the familiar, to the conventional, because we are uneasy in the presence of ambiguity.

What lies beyond convention is precisely that wonderful ambiguity in which the artist or the theoretician finds himself most at home. It is in this area that creative men play their great and commanding role, for it is the creative mind that dares to confront the obvious, that breaks through the bonds of accumulated distortions in perception, that tries to free itself from the strait-jackets of the conventional. The original mind *dares*—whether in the arts, or science, or philosophy—dares to look freshly. Original brains even dare to challenge the obvious; great minds transform it.

The history of physics is that of a science that moved along clumsily, slowly, crudely, and through models, built by bright men in their minds to clarify the phenomena they were busy studying. These models were always patched up, reinforced, revised, *made* to work—until someone came along who had the courage to ask a simple question, a remarkable and immensely creative question, which challenged, and in so doing sometimes destroyed, the prevailing model, to replace it with another.

"Creativity" is usually thought of as that rare, imaginative amalgam of talent and inspiration which gives us great paintings, poems, music, novels. The arts, that is, are assumed to be the magical province in which the creative afflatus flourishes. Only ignorance of science, of mathematics or physics, chemistry or engineering, permits so false a preconception. Consider: for thousands of years, human beings saw, as you and I see, that the sun rises in the east, crosses the heavens, and sinks into the west. We *see* this. There is no doubt of this. The sun moves. We see it move.

Yet some creative soul, long before Copernicus, asked himself this electrifying question: "But what if I *were on the sun?* If I were on the sun, might it not look as though it is the *earth* that is moving? Which one, in fact, is moving?"

Not until Newton did someone say *not,* "Why does the apple fall?" (they knew about gravity in those days), but, "Why does it fall *straight down,* as if toward the center of the earth, as the earth itself is moving?"

Newton proceeded to ask a series of questions which could be answered in only one way—a way which seemed absolutely fantastic: that the planetary system can be understood if all the great bodies act as if their entire gravitational pull, their entire mass, were *concentrated in one hypothetical pinpoint* at the center. Few feats of imagination have been as tremendous and world-shaking as this. Newton proceeded to work out the rules by which to maintain this hypothesis. And that work was saturated with ingenious correlations and original technique.

It was Darwin who asked, among other things, "Where does the human race come from?" It was Reimann and Lobachevsky who said, "But *is* a straight line really the shortest distance between two points—for instance, on a curved surface?" It was Rutherford who asked, "Can it be that inside the atom, this tiny, tiny, supposedly irreducible substance of matter, is a universe with a center and whirling bodies which duplicate the structure of the universe itself?"

But let us pause. None of these men really asked these questions in the way I have asked them. I think that we can better understand some of the problems they solved if we put them in the form of the kinds of questions I have suggested. In the case of Rutherford, for instance, he discovered the nucleus of the atom in 1911—and didn't know it. He wrote a letter to Hahn in 1913 in which he talked about the mathematical way of measuring the surprisingly large angle at which particles bounced off a thin metal screen, or foil; he was so absorbed in the relationship of these angles and distances to the imaginary center of the atom. It wasn't until Niels Bohr told him what he had discovered that Rutherford fully realized what was going on.

Or consider Einstein, who asked such questions as "But what do we mean by 'simultaneous'?" Are two things happening "simultaneously" if simply seen to be so? What of the position of the observer? What about observers in different positions— an event witnessed from the position of a man on a train moving *towards* lightning as against a man on the ground who is not moving?

Sigmund Freud really asked, "*Why* do people make mistakes in spelling, writing, talking? Can it be that there is a reason?"

Or, "What do dreams mean?"—not what do they predict, what possible magic or prescience is in them, but what is this particular person, in this dream, trying to say to himself? Is there a particular, special language in dreams?

Or, "Is it possible that we can love and hate the same object?"

Or, "Can it be that someone *does not know that he knows something?*" Can one part of the self be cut off from the remainder; and can it become known—not through reason, analyzing, deliberate effort, but through the deliberate avoidance of reason in a process of random associations, a process of symbolic, foolish, irrelevant, uncensored and unstructured verbal meanderings? Can we ever *not* be relevant?

Some years ago, in a talk to a group of psychoanalysts, I commented on the fact, so striking to me, that it took so very long for the human race to come upon, much less incorporate, ideas of this kind, and I read the following passage to them, "a passage you will all easily recognize":

Every man appears to have certain instincts, but in some persons they are subjected to the control of reason, and the better desires prevailing over them, they are either wholly suppressed or reduced in strength. I mean particularly those desires which are awake when the taming power of the personality is asleep, for it is in sleep that the wild beast in our nature stands up and walks about naked, and there is no conceivable folly or shame or crime, however unnatural, not excepting incest or parricide, of which such a nature may not be guilty. In all of us, even in good men, there is a latent wild beast which peers out in sleep.

I said to the psychoanalysts, "Of course you recognize this as coming from Sigmund Freud's book, *The Interpretation of Dreams*. But, alas, it was not written by Freud at all. It was written in the year 320 B.C.—by Plato." The coughing was eloquent.

Does it not seem remarkable to you that since all educated men in the past read a few books (there were not many books to read), surely thousands of them read Plato. Yet multitudes of years went by, and these words passed before how many eyes—but did not, to use a modern term, "register." History is full of similar examples.

As long ago as the twelfth century, bread mould was being used to cure inflamed abcesses.

The Chinese used ephedrine five thousand years ago.

The Hindus used snake-root for tranquilizers long, long before we had Miltown.

And among some primitive tribes in Africa, it has long been customary, when moving from one place to another, to take along some dirt—dirt from the floor of the old shelter, which is placed inside the new one to serve as an antibiotic. You may protest that these Africans could know nothing of microorganisms, but think only that they are propitiating the gods. Quite so.

And yet—was this propitiation, by any chance, linked to someone's observation that there was something about old dirt that protected against certain diseases, that gave the community protection against certain infections?

Our educational system does not teach people very well how to think, how to handle new concepts, how to solve problems. This is not only because the educational system is poor in imaginative techniques of pedagogy, but because even the wisest of us must make a very hard effort to revise the models with which we work—the only models we have.

We like to think of the physicist and the scientist as being men who quickly respond to the facts, the evidence, the new, promising clues to the future. Nonsense! Copernicus's heliocentric model offended not only the Church and faithful, but the greatest astronomer of his time, Tycho Brahe, who could not break with the tradition about the earth's lack of motion. He opposed Copernicus all his life.

Nineteenth-century scientists resisted the wave theory of light, enunciated by Thomas Young, because they were so completely wedded to the model of the corpuscular form of light.

Biologists resisted Pasteur's discovery that fermentation is not just a chemical process, and chemists resisted it as well.

Scientists resisted Lister's germ theory of disease. They also resisted Mendel's theory of genetic inheritance from 1865, when it was first announced, until the end of the century, because they just could not believe that individual, isolated characteristics were biologically transmitted.

The great Leibniz criticized Newton for failing to make "providential destiny" a part of his physical model.

And when Max Planck wrote his Ph.D. thesis for the University of Munich in 1879 and put into it entirely new ideas about the second law of thermodynamics, he later remarked, "None of my professors at the University had any understanding of its contents. I found no interest, let alone approval, even among the very scientists who were closely related to the topic. Helmholtz probably did not even read my paper at all, and Kirchoff expressly disapproved."

When Ernest Rutherford published *Radioactive Substances*

*and Their Radiation* in the year 1913, a book in which the structure of the atom (the idea that the atom has a nucleus with electrons spinning around it) was first spelled out, the book was reviewed in the excellent British journal *Nature* by a distinguished physicist of the time—and that review does not so much as touch upon the idea of atomic structure.

When Waterston suggested that gases have molecular aspects, his paper was rejected by the Royal Society; across page one is still written, "This paper is nothing but nonsense."

And when Poincaré, one of the great mathematicians of his day, examined Georg Cantor's contribution to mathematics, set theory, considered by mathematicians today as one of the great turning points in mathematical theory, he (Poincaré) said, "Later generations will regard this as a disease from which one has recovered."

The great Louis Agassiz remained one of the leading critics of Charles Darwin.

When Robert Chambers in 1840 published a book called *Messages of Creation,* in which he suggested a developmental view of the human story, Herschel, Owen, Agassiz, Huxley, Lyle, Murchison and others spoke against it.

When Karl Pearson in 1900 sent papers to the Royal Society in which he used statistics to analyze a problem in biology, a resolution of that society requested that, in the future, papers on biology should not contain mathematics.

When Roentgen announced X-rays, Lord Kelvin passed it off as a hoax. Kelvin also resisted the idea of the electronic composition of the atom. He just could not accept the idea that the atom was not indivisible.

Ampère's theory that there are electrical properties in the atom which have magnetic manifestations, was ignored by men who could not break beyond Newton's model.

Many assume that science can solve all problems, which is certainly not true. It is my conviction that the problems of human behavior are infinitely more complicated than any problems of physical sciences have thus far had to deal with. As I have said: How do we think? Where does an idea come from? How is an attitude formed? How can a prejudice be changed? What *is* love? What *is* aggression? What *is* insight? What *is* imagination?

It is the glory of the creative mind that it can leap over obstacles and complexities—to find, through insight or intuition or imagination, surprising solutions to problems which resist systematic or orderly solution. The tragedy of the *un*creative scholar is that he has spent so many years in autopsy that his mind has become a morgue.

I know no one more inept or obtruse than I am about the things I have been discussing here. I have no capacity to handle mathematics or work in the physical sciences. Everything in me groans when I see an equation, shudders when I run across a problem in mechanics.

But I have one characteristic which I cherish: I am prepared to believe anything. I may not *understand* it, but I have no anxieties about believing it—for the sake of where that belief may lead. I enjoy the game of "Let's suppose..." or "Let's pretend . . ." or "Just for the fun of it. . . ." or the magical "What if . . . ?"

Lest you think these are trivial formulations, may I point out to you that these are precisely the things that are involved in what we call scientific investigation—and surely in what we call the creative process. The capacity of the self to entertain (if only for a moment) absurd, irrational, outrageous, illogical, silly things; the capacity to get pleasure out of symbolic explorations—these are at the heart of the creative process. These plus daring, *daring* to ignore what you have been told is true, to ignore past rules and reason and logic, to court the unstructured chaos that rages below the surface of consciousness, to plunge into the unconscious without fear (though perhaps with anxiety, and often with ambivalence), to suspend sense.

Creativity, to me, is a shuttle between fancy and discipline, between imagination and system, between freedom and control, between fantasy and reason, between reverie and evidence, between imagination and analysis. It is a counterpoint, a kind of *ad libidum* internal dialogue in which one part of the self tries to communicate with the other parts of the self, in which the mind tries to break the restraints, the conventions, the crippling restrictions of what is proper or reasonable or sensible.

The history of science, or the arts, or philosophy, is the story of high points reached by men who had the courage to be infantile, to insist upon trying to wrest meanings from mysteries, to simplify complexity.

The operation of the mind in creative endeavor involves an incredible amount of loneliness and great stretches of what noncreative people are terrified of—uncertainty. There is a certain ambiguity always just beyond what is safe, what is known; I believe that the creative personality gets pleasure out of playing there, pleasure in the unstructured fantasy life, in the wild guess, the cherished hunch.

The most powerful displeasure, to the creative person, is boredom. Imagination, which is a leap into the unknown, is in part a flight from frustration.

Now you may think that all this is too abstract, that the counterpoint between reason and fantasy is something which we should try only after learning how to add, subtract, spell, think, etc.

But we are born into a *symbolic universe,* and we begin by thinking symbolically. Our first and only equipment for making sense, for locating regularity, for trying to understand form, sequence, identity, meaning is inchoate, wordless, preverbal.

Some years ago, I ventured to suggest that the world of the child is much closer to the world of Einstein than the world of Einstein is to the world of adults. I remember one Sunday afternoon telling my children, "I want to read you a thriller." It was a passage from Eddington's *The Physical World* and describes what happens when you take a step, according to nuclear physics. You are stepping from emptiness into emptiness; solidity is achieved by the bombardment of billions of electrons, and so on.

I read the passage—it wasn't more than 200 words—and said, "What do you think?"

My son, who was then twelve, said, "That sounds nutty!"

My daughter, who was then nine, said, "That upsets me."

My youngest, who was five, said, "But, of course, Daddy: *I play that game all the time.*"

Let me call your attention to the extraordinary experiments of Piaget with very small children, in which he tested their comprehension of space and motion as Einstein sees it. They were Einsteinians.

Copernicus offended men by daring to say that man is not the center of the world. Darwin came along and robbed us of the illusion of the uniqueness of our species. Freud came along and robbed us of control over our own souls. Harlow Shapley deflated the race by locating our galaxy, the last little hope of our egocentrism, way out, billions of heaven-knows-how-many-light-years away from the center of the universe. And now some people think that machines threaten to usurp or replace the uniqueness of the human mind. I am not among them.

We used to think that men could never devise machines that would do what the human brain can do. Today some think we have machines that will do, or do better, whatever men can do. Both views are silly. Ignorance about machines accounts for the optimism, and ignorance of human behavior accounts for the pessimism.

Machines certainly can solve problems, store information, scan and correlate and play games—but not with pleasure! And machines don't get bored; they don't dream; they have no reverie; they have no fantasy; they don't get excited; they don't get "inspired."

Machines don't grow as men grow; they don't change as men change; and *they can be set for single purposes.* There is almost no human activity which doesn't contain several goals, often in conflict.

We know less about human behavior than we know about animal behavior. We still have no satisfactory general theory of human intelligence, much less of human behavior. We know very little about the process by which you get an idea from one head into another.

To unlock the awesome power of the atom was as nothing, in my judgment, compared to what will happen when we at last unlock the power, the beauty, the daring, the infinite imaginativeness which still reside, in secret and untapped places, within the human mind and spirit.

# 12

---

## TELL ME NOT IN MOURNFUL NUMBERS

**P**lease read this couplet, which is historic, with care:

> Under a lamp the nude is vain.
> Broccoli is often blind.

And scan a second trail-blazing verselet:

> Life reached evilly through empty faces.
> Space flowed slowly o'er idle bodies.

These lyrical *pensées* are not the work of an idiot, or a brave new bard. The couplets are among the first to have come from (of all things) a digital computer. They were recorded for posterity by Mr. Wilbur Cross, several years ago.

Since then, the electronic-circuit kids have advanced to the astonishing point where they can program their mechanical genies to play Parcheesi, compose music, and even create paintings. (Numbers denote shape, color, position.)

The method for producing poems is quite simple, once you take three minutes to think about it. The programmers simply feed a basic vocabulary into the memory bank of their robot, making sure there is an ample assortment of parts of speech (verbs, articles, nouns, adjectives, prepositions, adverbs). Some words are "ranked" as openers of a sentence.

The operator of the computer, if asked to produce instant poesy, structures the syntax of a sentence by the sequence in which words are sucked out of the inventory. And so it is that digital computers can now replace Gertrude Stein, whose pigeons must by now be very dead on the grass, alas, my lass.

I was so carried away by visions of immortal odes-via-randomization that, owning no digital computer, I decided to conduct an experiment of my own. I wrote one hundred winged words on one hundred pretty slips of paper, making sure that about twenty percent of the words rhymed. Then I distributed the slips among twelve separate envelopes—marked, respectively:

> Openers
> Articles
> Adjectives
> Nouns
> Adverbs
> Verbs
> Adjectives
> Nouns
> Conjunctions
> Articles
> Verbs
> Nouns

Heart beating faster, I reached into the envelopes, in the same sequence as I have listed the categories above, and picked one slip out of each envelope. When I had extracted twenty words, I arranged them in four lines—and my heart broke the sound barrier. For what lay before me was this notable dithyramb:

> On bright pumpernickel gravely twinkle
> Sweet daffodils and a stately pickle,
> Where shrill brassieres shyly hide
> Broken dreams inside insides.

I am sending this to the Pulitzer Prize jury.

I now made a second venture into verse-via-envelope—this time adding a few verbs to my Openers. To my dismay (or delight), the slips I pulled out combined themselves to form this pregnant Thought for Our Times:

> Hail the hairy artichoke!
> Torquemada's frog will gloat.
> Can lunatics like noodle toys?
> Angels have no adenoids.

Can you blame me for taking a swan-dive into the golden cache once more?

> How deftly pink suspenders sigh
> A pox on clavichords that lie.
> Hark, hark!   The dawn barks Gosh!
> And pregnant mice sell succotash.

Do you want to scale Parnassus, too? It's quite easy. Just follow the rules I've given you. Choose glowing, gleaming words. Don't worry about gibberish, *non-sequiturs,* or oxymorons.

I don't care whether moon shots may not be resumed until 2035. It's worth waiting that long to gain lunar provenance for something as throat-grabbing as this, my latest madrigal:

> Swish green albino dust
> Through atavars unborn
> And circumcise the circumscribed
> Circumstance: Juno stabbed the rooster.

I have read that over many times. It is very beautiful, and makes no sense.

### L'Envoi

Do you think I am poking fun at electronic devices, or the New, Liberated Poesy? Please believe me when I say: I certainly am.

# 13

## YOU HAVE A RIGHT TO BE UNHAPPY

Once upon a time (very long ago) a man could stare glumly out a window, or grunt at his wife, or slam the door, or stalk off on a solitary walk, without having his loved ones rush to his rescue with bright psychiatric phrases and psychotherapy handy-dandy.

Once upon a time (believe it or not) we were not silly enough to expect everyone to walk around in a state of bliss, or meet every crisis with a wholesome grin, or give hourly demonstrations of being "well adjusted."

Once upon a time (oh blessed time!) sensible men simply knew that life, even at best, is beset with difficulties, that frustration or disappointment or defeat is natural and as inevitable as changes in the weather.

There was a time, in short, when we all had the good sense to realize that discontent, despair, even failure are normal, that squabbles—between men and women, parents and children —are unavoidable; that not everybody was intended by God, or fate, or biochemistry to be contented all of the time. We even had the good sense to know that anyone who is happy all the time is nuts. One of the marks of good sense and good health is precisely the capacity to be unhappy when reality warrants it—to be unhappy soundly, without apology or rationalization. We knew, that is, that life never was and never can be a gigantic bowl of cherries. We knew it is folly to try to induce happiness by exhortation or reprimand, or by hints about the wonders of psychoanalysis or Zen Buddhism.

But all this has changed. Pollyannas* walk proudly through every suburb of the land now, carrying symbolic banners which proclaim that discontent is unnecessary, unnatural, and un-American. We have all become skittish about being labeled "neurotic." We are all besieged by euphoric optimists who strain at the leash to "help" us. It has gotten so that you can't have an ingrown toenail without suffering the vehement charity of other people's "insight." (If you don't have insight, it's a pretty suspicious sign, probably a defense against "repressed hostilities" or "latent homosexuality," which are a lot more common than housemaid's knee.)

Now all this is something quite new in man's experience. As recently as thirty years ago, no one questioned your right to be unhappy. "The pursuit of happiness" was only one of the worthy goals in life. Men took it for granted that there are rewards in working, in trying, in failing, in cursing, in trying again. Happiness was considered a blessing, not a guarantee. Men were granted the dignity of periodic discontent. They were permitted to suffer pain or fall into moods or seek solitude without having every sigh promptly analyzed, "interpreted," dissected, and discussed. Today, alas, a mood is not a mood: it is a "symptom." A defeat is not a defeat; it is a sign of an "unconscious wish to fail." We no longer have whims: we are slaves to "motivations."

---

* Pollyanna was the name of a sweet young girl in a novel by Eleanor H. Porter, an American writer. The name is now used to describe anyone who is always optimistic. My publisher insists that I explain this.

I think I am safe in saying that never in history have so many people known exactly what is wrong with everyone else. The social air is crowded with diagnostic jargon and therapeutic exhortations. Dear friends confuse our discontent with disease and mistake simple displeasure for dark disturbance. And even our mildest demurrers to the Florence Nightingales of the psyche who besiege us are dubbed "Resistance!"— which *proves* how much you really, despite your protestations, need "help." Few people have the gall to operate on your liver, but just as few show the slightest hesitancy about messing with your "unconscious."

Don't misunderstand me: I am not criticizing the psychiatrists or psychoanalysts. It is their function, and a useful one, to try to heal the sick. What I am inveighing against are the new clichés that conclude that if you aren't ecstatic you're sick, and the new idiocy which assumes that anyone who has gone to a psychiatrist or read three books about psychoanalysis is ipso facto qualified to decide who is, in fact, sick and what magical incantations must be invoked to heal him.

Every so often young people, mistaking my years for wisdom and my height for maturity, ask me for Advice. Aside from trotting out the hoary truisms that most experience boils down to, I offer them only this: "Diminish your demands, especially on others."

To the gallant husband or doting wife who can't sleep because of the other's "conflict" or depression, the best I can say is this: "Love him (or her)—and let her (or him) alone. Let him enjoy his troubled moments. He may need occasional withdrawal or self-inquiry. Don't intrude upon the private mood: it does not necessarily mean he hates you or resents his mother or should be carted off to the couch."

Balance, proportion, good sense—surely these are better than hasty psychologizings. The confidence that a mood will pass, that some things simply take time, that not everything needs to be explained or debated, may be a good deal more desirable than unsolicited missions of salvation. A soul in distress is not necessarily doomed.

We have all been bamboozled into thinking that it is our sacred duty to "understand." This is nonsense. There is a good deal about others, even those we know well, that we will never understand too well. It is enough to know that each of us is often irrational, petulant, childish, and unfair. The why is less important than the effort to keep others from suffering because of us.

Whosoever is human must reconcile himself to being imperfect. We must surrender our infantile dream that anyone really lives happily ever after. To even the most successful and "well adjusted" of us, a large part of life involves duties that are dull and routines that are disagreeable.

Happiness is rare, not common. Bliss, save in precious and transient moments, is an invention of poets, clung to by genuine neurotics. If we spent less time trying to have "fun" we might discover the endless rewards and resources of that internal self which is at home with contemplation and solitude, which can accept disappointment or ungratified desire. Only the very young or the hopelessly naive expect life to give them everything they hoped for, or dreamed of, or read about.

Fairy tales, at least, were labeled tales; the heroes and heroines were saved by luck or virtue or magic. It is one of the unhappy (but not so terrible) facts of life that virtue does not always prevail, that fate is utterly indifferent about how and when it doles out fortune, and that Pollyanna was a pretty silly, to say nothing of tiresome, little girl.

# 14

## A DANDY WAY TO SAVE YOUR
## MARRIAGE—OR ANYONE ELSE'S

**W**hy do we call our times the Age of Anxiety? I think we live in the Age of Advice. Too much advice. Brisk, confident, aggressive (and infuriating) Advice.

We are navel-deep in professional counselors, expert psychologists, "trained" advisors. I put quotation marks around "trained" because people assume that training guarantees competence. It does not. How many of the earnest souls trained in Education are good teachers? How many Ph.D.s in Economics understand how a society—any society—really works? How many psychoanalysts are happily married? ...

You can't pick up a paper or magazine, turn on your radio or TV, without being assaulted by energetic admonitions on everything from diets to orgasms. In an outpouring of encouragements not seen since Dr. Coué's phenomenally popular "Every-day-in-every-way-I-am-getting-better-and-better!" (a declamatory cure for everything from headaches to transvestitism) we are being drowned in vulgarized psychiatry: tips on stammering and cures for frigidity; how to understand menopausal depression or the masculine yen for porno flicks; what to tell Junior about masturbation or Missy about her crush on a female hockey coach.

Perhaps the most flourishing field in the Tower of Helpful Babel is Marriage Counseling. I was mildly skeptical of the gurus in this special art until the other day, when I lunched with an old classmate, Ben—let's call him Outré.

Ben and Sybil Outré are the happiest couple I've ever known. They met fourteen years ago and promptly fell in love. Their courtship was glorious, their romance unclouded. In seven months they were married—and ever since, they have been the joy and envy of everyone who knows them.

Ben is a reporter for the New York ———; Sybil is a designer for the ——— Mills. They have no children, which may account for the absence of wrinkles around their eyes and the presence of laugh lines around their mouths.

All in all, which is about as far as anyone can go, Ben and Sybil Outré are shining examples of the power and persistence of Love.

I'm telling you all this because when I lunched with Ben I could not help expressing my pleasure in knowing of a marriage so rare and felicitous.

Ben smiled.

Something about that smile disturbed me. "What does that mean?" I asked.

"What?"

"The Mona Lisa bit."

"Okay." Ben grinned. "Shall I tell you the real secret of our perfect marriage?"

"Your sex life is superb," I ventured.

"No. It *is* superb, but that's not the reason."

"You screw the tops back on toothpaste tubes, and Sybil doesn't wear curlers to bed."

"Naw."

"You let Sybil refurnish the apartment whenever she—"

"Heaven forfend."

I had exhausted my supply of real reasons for a Perfect Marriage. "I give up."

"Helmut Küchenpflammer," said Ben.

"Gesundheit!"

He leaned back and smiled evilly. "Dr. Küchenpflammer. He is a marriage counselor."

"*Don't* tell me," I told him, "that you and Sybil actually went to consult one of *those!*"

"It is he who made our marriage perfect."

"How?" I gulped.

"By recommending that we get a divorce."

There was no feather nearby for you to knock me over with. Cheerfully, Ben proceeded to tell me—I'll write it without quotation marks.

For the first eight wonderful years of marriage (said Ben), Sybil and I lived in utter bliss. We adored each other's humor, enjoyed each other's friends, threw parties that, I think you will agree, were as delightful as any in Manhattan.

*No* couple ever got more out of New York. We had season tickets to the opera. We devoured the theater. We ate in superlative restaurants. Every Sunday morning we breakfasted on bagels and heavenly cream-cheese-and-lox. Sunday afternoons we walked in the park, or through Greenwich Village, or along the East River.

All this for eight long, precious years.... Then—well, I suppose anything I say now would only be surface stuff (but think how much we live on surfaces). We started to get on each other's nerves. I'd snap at Sybil for interrupting my reveries, and she'd snap at me for not paying attention to hers. She found excuses for not going to Japanese movies, so I moodily went alone; I resisted meeting her at Parke-Bernet, so she testily went by herself.

We'd bicker over everything: Why didn't I want to drive up to the Berkshires? Why didn't she want to go to Bermuda? Why didn't I wash my soup bowl instead of letting it soak in the sink? Why did she always take pencils from my desk? She wanted to walk briskly when I wanted to dawdle. She dieted when I wanted to gorge. We were simply rubbing each other's sensibilities raw.

It was Sybil who brought up the name of Dr. Küchenpflammer.

I laughed—not at his name (my God, you have to admire a
man who has not changed such a handle to "Cook"!), but at
the idea of people like us traipsing to a marriage mechanic. "Absurd," I said. "Idiotic."

At two o'clock the next day I was sitting before him with
Sybil.

We took turns cataloguing our grievances. Dr. Küchenpflammer listened. He nodded.

He was not impressive, I must tell you. He just listened and
nodded. He nodded to what I said, which pleased me, and he
nodded to what Sybil said, which didn't.

After half an hour, Dr. Küchenpflammer took over. "I think
I understand your problem." (He spoke without a shred of ac-
cent, it grieves me to report.) "I see three possible solutions. . . .
First, and most obvious: Get a divorce."

"Oh, *no*," Sybil stammered.

"Hell no." I flushed.

"Very well. Solution Two: Remain married."

Sybil spluttered, "But we're not *happy* together!"

I fumed, "Our marriage *isn't working out!*"

She retorted, "He's wrapped up in his infantile needs!"

I declaimed, "She's so damned un*rea*sonable!"

Dr. Küchenpflammer raised a minatory hand. "Which brings
us to Solution Three: Get a divorce—but go right on living
together."

After locating my voice I said icily, "*That* is a contradiction
in terms!"

"Only if you are a slave to terminology," the doctor leered.

"But how can you expect me to divorce and then live with a
man I love but can't *stand??*" cried Sybil.

"That goes double for me!" I thundered.

Dr. Küchenpflammer smiled, rather pityingly. "Consider. You
get a divorce. But you keep your present apartment. Then you
rent another, smaller, much less comfortable place—to which

either of you can go whenever you are furious with the other or need to storm out in righteous anger. You can, if you wish, call that refuge 'Achilles' Tent.' "

Sybil stammered, "But what good will that *do?*"

I growled, "What good will *that* do?"

Dr. Küchenpflammer raised both hands this time. "Loads and loads of good. The fact—unfortunate, but true—is that marriage kills romance. My Solution Three restores the latter by periodically 'terminating' the former. *Think* for a moment! The fact that you will no longer be married means that neither of you will feel you *own* the other. You will not be chained to marital duties—to submit, to surrender, to attack. Since you will not be married, you will pay more attention to each other, be more sensitive to the other's desires, more careful to step around emotional minefields. And because you know you (or he, or she) can flee in a huff to Achilles' Tent, you will not wreck your relationship (as so many people do) by staying together only because there is no place to which either of you can conveniently escape!

"It is salubrious for a couple to separate periodically. In your case—well, the romantic streak in each of you is too powerful, which means it is too weak to endure the prolonged strains of life. Especially life in the United States, where we have all been deluded into thinking that since human behavior can be understood by experts, it *must* be understood by loved ones. It simply flabbergasts me to see how many husbands who can't understand Aesop expect their wives to act like Aristotle, and how many wives who can't do long division expect their husbands to understand menopausal depression."

"I am *years* away from the menopause!" Sybil glared.

"So am I!" snapped I.

"I just was trying to say something fresh about empathy." Dr. Küchenpflammer sighed. "Achilles' Tent is where each of you will find periodic respite from the voracity of your partner's demands. Whenever one of you walks out on the other, your pride will be fed, your face saved, your sense of justice fortified.

And when you return from Achilles' Tent, romance will blossom and flourish anew—no matter which of you first finishes wallowing in noble remorse. Of course, you could *both* leave, and go to the refuge together"—he grinned—"but I told you it must be smaller and much less attractive than your common, beautiful, totally illicit home."

Ben Outré ended: "Well, buddy, we did just that."

"You mean you and Sybil aren't *married?!*" I cried.

"We were divorced six years ago," Ben smiled. "And we have been deliriously happy together ever since."

If you ask me, that's the most intelligent statement about marriage I have heard in my whole life.

In fact, I used Dr. Küchenpflammer's exact words, "Marriage kills romance!" as I put *my* wife on the plane to Reno.

"Find a crummy apartment!" my mate called, blowing me a kiss.

# 15

## ALL HAIL, TRANSLATORS!

homas Huxley once said that new ideas begin as heresies and end as superstitions. What is just as intriguing to me is the number of new ideas which, after the shock of their novelty has worn off, turn out to be revelations of the obvious.

I was bogged down in a stretch of translation not long ago when a banality suddenly struck me with the force of a revolutionary illumination: What we know of the history and literature of other peoples is almost entirely the product of translations. A tremendous portion of our education and our store of knowledge comes from, and is rooted in, translated works.

Except for a handful of scholars and multilinguists, how many of us can (or did) read Tacitus in Latin or Thucydides in Greek? How many of us could tackle the original texts of Herodotus or Confucius, Voltaire or Goethe, Cervantes or Dostoevsky—to say nothing of Babylonian records, the *Bhagavad Gita,* or the *Tale of Genji?*

Translators, once you think of it, have played a monumental role in human affairs. Interpreters may properly be called the carriers of civilization and its first cross-fertilizers. Trade, travel, the contact of cultures—all depended on interpreters.

Or take the great books of philosophy, science, geography, astronomy, medicine. . . . The words of Euclid, Aristotle, Aristarchus of Samos (who held that the earth revolves on its own axis *and* moves around the sun), Plato, Galen—they were unknown to Europeans (except a small band of savants) until the twelfth and thirteenth centuries. That's when those historic works were translated into Latin—from Arabic, into which tongue they had been rendered from Syriac (!), into which language they had been translated from the Greek. These texts were thrice removed from the original, riddled with inaccuracies, but they flowed into Europe's monasteries and universities to transform the world.

I need hardly wax eloquent about the influence of books in the civilization of the West. A moment's rumination reminds us that it was translations of Plutarch and Suetonius that provided kings and princes with priceless lessons from the lives, reigns or misfortunes of their predecessors in the pageant of power. It was from translations of Machiavelli that Anglo-Saxon and Nordic and Slavic rulers learned diabolic refinements of statecraft, politics, diplomacy. It was from translations of Castiglione that many a royal court learned etiquette and elegant manners.

The poets of the Renaissance, the playwrights of Elizabethan England, French, Italian, Spanish humanists were profoundly influenced by their readings of the classics (Homer, Aristophanes, etc.)—in translation. Ben Jonson tells us Shakespeare "had small Latin and less Greek," yet based six of his plays on Greek history and six of his greatest on Roman.

Suppose I make the point another way: Had translations never been made, would Augustine or Vergil, Erasmus or Montaigne or Cervantes be recognized outside of a few universities?

Were translations forbidden, what could you or I know of Carthage or Cathay? Of the Mongol dynasts, or the Pharaohs, or old Kyoto? Of the Muslims, the Venetians, the Vikings? Or even what happened this morning in Peking, Moscow, Tokyo, Jerusalem?

But what we do know about history is marred by astonishing errors—because of translation. The Italians say *"traduttore traditori"*: Translators are traitors. The gibe is cruel, but educational. Take a simple example: Do our history books tells us that, actually, Greek tyrants were not tyrannical? Histories should tell us that, for among the ancient Greeks, a tyrant (*tyrannos*) was simply someone who had seized power. Many Greek tyrants were quite liberal, popular, and very far from being tyrannical. But somewhere along the line of translated renditions, the word *tyrannos* lost its neutral meaning and became invidious.

Now take a more important body of errors in translation, if one contemplates the consequences: the Bible. The story here is mind-boggling. For instance: Moses never had horns on his head; the Israelites did not cross the Red Sea; the three Wise Men were not wise men; the ... but let me hold off until later.

I first became aware of the farrago of boners in English translations of Holy Scripture when I spent a year studying comparative religion in the Divinity School at the University of Chicago. (I had not the slightest intention of becoming a divine, divine though the idea may sound; I was simply fascinated by the varieties of men's faith and the underlying psychology of religious belief.)

I was astonished to learn such simple but startling facts as these: the Bible (from the Greek *biblia*) is a collection of "little books"; these books were not written at one time and not by one man, but by a good many men across a stretch of at least 1300 years—starting 1200 years before the birth of Jesus. The holy books were gathered together in haphazard fashion down the centuries—according to the judgment or whims of religious leaders, rabbis, kings, priests. The Bible was not even called "Bible" until the sixteenth century, and not "Holy" until 1568! (These facts floored me.)

The immortal King James version (1611) was the *third* English translation authorized. The Wycliff Bible (*ca.* 1388) was branded heretical by the Church. William Tyndale's great translation of 1525 so fixed the English style and mood of the

Bible that all later versions "must be looked upon as revisions . . . not independent translations." Yet Tyndale was killed. . . .*

From 1611 to 1697, the New Testament was revised seven different times. A revised Revised Version appeared in 1885, and at least twenty different translations have appeared since then.

I was shocked to discover how many solemn passages in the Old and New Testaments were printed in a form misleading or downright *wrong,* when compared with the earliest Hebrew/Aramaic/Greek manuscripts.

The glorious King James version used a late sixteenth-century idiom that was outmoded by the time that great Bible was printed. The prose lends incomparable charm to the text—and discombobulating ambiguity.

What on earth is meant by "Ye are not straitened in us"?

Or take the misleading references to money. A *penny* was not a trifle to the Hebrews; it was the going rate for twelve hard hours of work.

Or take the incorrect impressions of time: "The third hour" leads a modern reader to think that what is meant is 3:00 A.M. or 3:00 P.M.; but what "the third hour" really meant was the third hour after dawn, *i.e.,* eight or nine in the morning.

In many unhappy cases the original meaning of a word is *opposite* the meaning assigned it by King James's scholars. The phrase *by and by* meant, to the Hebrews, not "in a little while" but "immediately." And to the King Jamesians, *comprehend*

---

* Tyndale's story is as instructive as it was tragic. He started to translate the New Testament, but found such hostility to this in England that he went to Germany. A church injunction stopped him in Cologne; he moved to Worms. Copies of his translation reached England in 1526 and were at once denounced and suppressed by the bishops. Cardinal Wolsey sent out an order to Worms to have Tyndale arrested. Tyndale worked in a hideaway and published his translation of the Pentateuch in 1530. Wolsey's agents captured Tyndale in Antwerp. He was tried for heresy—and strangled, then burned at the stake, on orders of Emperor Charles V. I tell you all this to illustrate the perils that translators (the most innocent of men) have often confronted.

signified not "comprehension," as we assume, but "overcoming an obstacle."

Or take *candles* and *candlesticks:* They were unknown to the Hebrews, who used torches or oil lamps.

*Servant* in the Bible often should be "slave." Slavery was rife in the ancient world.

To "add one cubit unto his stature" (Matthew 6:27) is ludicrous: a cubit is eighteen inches.

I hate to think of how many people have been slaughtered, or idealistically slaughtered others, because of some error in the translation of one or another passage in one or another "holy" text. But one can hardly avoid being amused by the mistakes made (inevitably) in printing our Bible.

In the time of Charles I, a pious printer rendered Psalm 14:1 as "The fool hath said in his heart that there is a God." Copies of that edition were frantically suppressed.

In 1611, a Bible used *Judas* instead of *Jesus* in Matthew 26:36, making the passage read "Judas then came with his disciples to a place called Gethsemane."

In 1823, a Bible had Rebekah rising not with the lovely "damsels," but with (no doubt puzzled) "camels." That work became known as the Camel's Bible.

In an edition of Scripture in 1806, the fishers of Ezekiel 47:10 suffered a gruesome fate: their *r* was dropped—so the fishers became fishes, which gave us this tantalizing image: "And it shall come to pass that the fishes shall stand upon it." Who can blame churchmen for dubbing this The Standing Fishes Bible?

The most sacrilegious, scandalous of all printings, known among the cognoscenti as The Wicked Bible (1631), actually rendered the seventh commandment as "Thou shalt commit adultery."

What a pity Freud was not around to comment.

Earlier, I teased your expectations by puncturing traditional images of Moses, the Israelites crossing the Red Sea, the Three Wise Men. Let me now give you the evidence:

*The horns on the head of Moses.*

Think of Michelangelo's statue, or of a thousand paintings and drawing of Moses. . . . But those nubby tips of horns on the immortal brow were put there because of a mistake in translation. In Genesis, Moses is described as coming down from Sinai with *karan* (Hebrew for "rays of light" or "emanations") shining from his head. In the fourth century, St. Jerome, making his historic Latin version of the Bible, the so-called Vulgate edition, mistook the Hebrew word *karan* for *karen*. Reading that tiny *e* instead of *a* gave Moses horns: that's what *karan* means.

*The Israelites and the Red Sea.*

"Red Sea" is a flagrant error in translation. The Israelites, fleeing from their pursuers, did not cross the Red Sea. They were nowhere near the Red Sea at the time.

What the Israelites crossed, in modern translations, is the Sea of Reeds or The Sea of Bulrushes, either of which is accurate English for the Hebrew *Yam Suf* of the ancient texts. (I wish I could say the error made was mistaking Reed Sea for Red Sea!) The change to Sea of Reeds offers us a crutch for credibility. After all, the rushes in a marsh will "part" more readily, without divine intervention, than the waters of a sea. (But how were the pursuing Egyptians then drowned?) The Sea of Reeds is 100 to 125 miles from the northern tip of the Red Sea.

*The Three Wise Men.*

Translators made a mistake in Matthew when they rendered *magos* (Greek) or *magi* (Latin) as "wise men." The word in the text means astrologers, soothsayers, dream-interpreters—even sorcerers. (Our "magician" and "magic" come from *magi,* the plural of *magus.*)

Nor does the New Testament tell us that there were *three* "wise men." No number is given.

Of much greater importance and consequence are the astonishing changes in the translations of gospel made and jointly agreed upon after decades of work and discussion by a committee of scholars: Protestant, Catholic, Jewish. Consider the substantive magnitude of such revisions as these, the product of immense and impeccable scholarship:

"In the beginning, God created the heaven and the earth" is now given in several modern translations as: "When God began to create the heaven and the earth." (Obviously, God existed before He created anything.)

The Third Commandment now reads: "Thou shalt not swear falsely by the name of the Lord your God; for the Lord will not clear one *who swears falsely* by His name" (my italics). The change is of cardinal importance, for in the new translations, man is commanded to avoid *perjury,* not profanity—which the King James "take the name of the Lord in vain" seemed to signify.

The most historic change, surely, has been made in Isaiah 7:14 (and therefore in Matthew 1:22–23, which quotes Isaiah 7:14). The King James Bible, as do bibles in 1431 different translations, recounts how Isaiah promised Hezekiah (a king of the Jews, who was defending himself against two enemy armies) that his aggressors will be destroyed:

Therefore the Lord himself shall give you a sign:
Behold, a virgin shall conceive, and bear a son. . . .

But new translations render this passage as:

Therefore the Lord himself shall give you a sign: A
young woman is with child, and she will bear a son. . . .

The word Isaiah used was *almah,* which in Hebrew does not mean "virgin." It means "young woman." (The Hebrew word for virgin is *betulah.*) Isaiah used the word he meant, which Greek and Latin translators misinterpreted.

New translations of the Bible have been inspired by the dramatic discovery of ancient documents that predate all earlier manuscripts; the most famous and significant, of course, are the Dead Sea Scrolls. And the new translations agree on the corrections I have sketched above.

Before you vent too much wrath on errant scribes and scholars, consider with charity the pitfalls that make any translator's life a misery.

A language is a *Weltanschauung*. Even languages very close in origin develop surprising differences. The English "conscience" is not the same as the French *conscience* (which means consciousness or conscientiousness). German had no word for bully until the twentieth century (a mordant comment on Teutonic values) and can only render the Englishman's idea of "fair play" as " 'fair' *Spielen*."

If this be true of tongues so close to each other in birth, so laden with cognates, so cross-fertilized by usage and literature, how much more does it intrude when one tries to translate Aramaic or Hebrew into Latin, Greek—or English?

The most tormenting aspect of translation is this: What is idiomatic in one tongue is idiotic in another. Think for a moment of what happens if a translator of English is not savvy enough about colloquialisms to know that "Tell it to Sweeney" is a rebuff, not a request; that a Northern Spy may have been an undercover agent for Ulysses S. Grant—or only a variety of apple; that Jack-in-the-pulpit does not mean the preacher's name is Jack; that behind the eight-ball is gibberish in most of the world.

Perfectly sensible Russian physicists believe that the first nuclear atomic pile in history was constructed in a pumpkin field—that being the Russian translation of "squash court," which was the site in the concrete bowels of the stadium (Stagg *Field*) at the University of Chicago.

Can one blame a Russian scientist-translator for that boner? Why, even a sophisticated Japanese translated "out of sight, out of mind" as "Those distant are insane."

"A good translation," said Benedetto Croce, "is a work of art."

I think it is also a feat of wide knowledge, perception, rare sensitivity—and anthropology.

# 16

---

## TEN PARABLES

**M**y favorite revelations of truth are to be found in parables—tales which have a meaning and point a moral. Thousands of them have come down to us through the centuries, and they are as fresh as the day when they were first told.

Here I have chosen ten parables which seem to me to capture the essence of different cultures or faiths.

Because what is merely different often strikes us as "peculiar," I have adapted these stories freely—condensing and rewriting them, so that they fall into that particular form, the anecdote with a "punch line," which we of the West love.

### Truth and Parable
#### (Hebrew)

An old rabbi, famed for his great learning, was asked why he so often drove home a philosophical point by telling a story. "That," he said, smiling, "I can best explain—through a story."

This is the story he then told:

There was a time, long ago, when Truth walked about on

earth unadorned, as naked as his name. And whoever of God's children encountered Truth swiftly turned away and gave him no welcome.

So Truth wandered throughout many lands and many people, hoping to be recognized and loved; but he was always rebuffed and rejected. As the decades passed, Truth grew more and more despondent, and less and less sure of his worth.

One day, Truth met Parable, who was strolling along happily in tinkling finery and many-colored garb.

"Ah, Parable," sighed Truth, "how happy you seem!"

"I am," smiled Parable. "But what makes *you* so gloomy?"

"I am ugly," said Truth.

"You? Ugly? Nonsense! Why do you say such a thing?"

"Because no matter where I go, God's children are repelled and turn away from me!"

Parable said, "That is not why they avoid you.... Here— borrow my clothes. See what happens then."

So Truth donned Parable's lovely garments—and lo! Everywhere he appeared, he was greeted with pleasure and welcomed with delight.

The old rabbi ended his story with a chuckle: "The Truth is that men simply cannot bear to face Truth. They will only recognize him when he comes prettily disguised."

## The Coward and the Philosopher
### (Muslim)

A pasha was crossing the sea in a fine ship when a terrible storm arose. One of the Persian slaves, who had never been off land before, began to weep and moan, and he cried out in such bursts of terror that no one could reassure him.

The pasha called out angrily, "Is there no one aboard who can quiet this disgusting coward?"

A philosopher, who happened to be on the vessel, said, "With your permission, sire, I think I can quiet him." "Proceed!" said the pasha.

The philosopher observed the chattering slave and summoned several sailors. "Throw this wretch into the water."

They threw the slave into the sea, where he began to drown, thrashing around wildly, and his screams were terrible to hear.

"Now pull him back," said the philosopher.

The sailors hauled the slave back onto the ship. He clung to the deck, panting, frightened—but silent.

The pasha asked the philosopher, "How do you explain this?"

To which the wise man replied, "Before he had a taste of drowning, he could not appreciate the safety of a ship."

To the angels in Paradise, Purgatory is Hell;
But to the doomed of Hell, Purgatory is Paradise.*

### The Diplomat and the King
(Chinese)

When Yentze, famed and witty diplomat from the state of Ch'i, was appointed ambassador to the kingdom of Ch'u, the King of Ch'u, knowing that Yentze was as proud in spirit as he was short in stature, decided to take him down a peg or two. The king had a small opening knocked out of the city walls, next to the great entrance gate, and told his captain of the guard to order Yentze to crawl through "the dog gate" when he appeared to present his credentials to the king.

When Yentze arrived at the city walls, the captain of the guard said, "My king orders you to enter through the dog gate."

Yentze bowed. "One uses a dog gate in a dog country," he said. "I cannot insult the great land of Ch'u by entering in any way save through the great, grand gate so appropriate to your king."

When this was reported to the king, he commanded that Yentze be brought before him at once.

The king surveyed the diplomat coolly, and, seeking to em-

---

* This story is taken from the *Gulistan,* a reader used in Mohammedan schools. The *Gulistan,* part prose, part poetry, was written by Sadi, a Persian poet of the 13th century. It is a compendium of proverbs, legends, sermons and moralistic episodes.

barrass him anew, said, "Ch'i must be as scanty in population as its people are short in body, if they were obliged to send you here."

"Nay, sire, my country is most populous," said Yentze, smiling, "and its people renowned for splendor of body and mind. But in Ch'i we select our ambassadors according to the worth of the country to which they are assigned. And I—as Your Majesty so swiftly perceived—am the shortest and least clever man in Ch'i."

### The Wisdom of John
#### (Christian)

When the beloved apostle John was getting on in years, his young disciples would sit in a circle before him each morning and hear from him a sermon about the life and the teachings of Christ. Then the young disciples would go forth to preach the gospel, one by one, wherever they could find men to listen.

Each day the young disciples drew from John's words some central thought; and each day they went forth, seeking converts, and built their message around the thought John had given them. Year by year they spread the word and saw the faithful multiply.

One day, a group of new and eager disciples came to John and asked, "What truth do you give us to carry now to the people?"

The apostle John was silent, lost in thought, and the young men waited expectantly. At last John spoke. "Tell the people this: 'Children, love ye one another.'"

The young disciples regarded each other unhappily.

"Why are you displeased?" asked John.

"We have often told the people this!" exclaimed one disciple.

"We have preached love again and again!" said another.

"Can you not give us something more?" begged a third.

John shook his head. "No, for there *is* nothing more. This is what you must—now and forever—tell all men is our Savior's message: 'Children, you *must* love one another.'"

### The Tiger and the Tyrant
(Confucian)

Confucius was walking through the countryside with one of his disciples when they saw a woman weeping beside a new grave. "Why do you cry so bitterly?" Confucius asked.

"Because of the tiger," replied the woman.

"What tiger?"

"The terrible tiger who comes down from the hills," said the distraught woman. "First he killed my father; then he killed my husband; and now he has killed my only son."

"Then why do you not leave this fearful place?" asked Confucius.

The woman looked at him in surprise. "But here there is no tyrant."

Confucius turned to his disciple. "Mark her words, lad: A tyrant is indeed worse than the fiercest tiger."


### Whom Did Jesus Flee?*
(Sufi)

A peasant once saw Jesus running toward a mountain, so the peasant ran alongside and called out, "O noble one, why are you running? No one is chasing you."

Jesus said nothing, but ran on.

"But are you not the Messiah?" the peasant exclaimed. "Are you not the one who restored sight to the blind? The one who speaks over the dead and makes them rise?"

Jesus paused. "Yes."

"Then you, who can do whatever you want, what can you possibly fear?"

---

* This story is adapted from the *Mathnawi* of Rumi (A.D. 1207–1273). The *Mathnawi*, called "verily a Koran of the Persians," is a huge book by the Sufi master and poet, Jelel Uddin Rumi, which contains hundreds of sermons, poetic verses, legends, homilies, and lives of the saints. (Incidentally, the Whirling Dervishes belong to the Sufi sect.) The *Mathnawi* has been translated into English by R. A. Nicholson and A. J. Auberry.

Jesus sighed. "Through God can I pronounce spells over the blind, or over corpses—and bring them back to life. But with fools I have pleaded—lovingly, hundreds of times—and it was no cure for their folly. ... It is the fool from whom I flee."

### The Beggar and the Wallet
(Jewish)

A beggar wandered into a village, cold and hungry, and heard that the richest man there had lost his wallet and offered a reward of ten rubles to whoever found and returned it.

The beggar prayed: "O Lord, if I could only find that wallet ... if I could only win that reward...."

He went through the streets, searching high and low, and—miracle of miracles—found the wallet. There were ninety rubles in it. The beggar ran to the rich man's house. "Sir! Your wallet! I found it—and have come for the reward."

The rich man opened the wallet, counted the money, and with a cunning smile said, "There were one hundred rubles in this wallet, and now I find only ninety. You stole ten rubles—and you have the gall to ask for a reward?! Begone, thief, before I throw you out."

The beggar fled, sore at heart, and searched out the village rabbi. "O rabbi," he wept, "a misfortune has befallen me. I am a beggar, but not a thief...." He told the rabbi what had happened.

The rabbi, who well knew the rich man's character, sat in silence for a while, deep in thought, then asked one of his disciples to summon the rich man.

When the rich man entered the rabbi's house and saw the beggar, he turned to the rabbi indignantly. "Did you call me here because of this scoundrel?"

"Yes. He has told me what happened. He swears he did not steal ten rubles from your wallet."

"Whom will you believe?" demanded the rich man. "This filthy beggar or me?"

"I will believe you, of course," said the rabbi. "May I see the wallet?"

The rich man handed the wallet to the rabbi, who gave it to the beggar. "Go; it is yours."

"Rabbi, what are you *doing?*" cried the rich man.

"Taking your word," said the rabbi. "Obviously, the wallet this poor man found, containing only ninety rubles, can't be the one you lost ... so we shall wait until someone finds the wallet with one hundred rubles in it."

### The Dream
(Chinese)

Chuang Tze, the sage, said, "Once I dreamed that I was a butterfly. I followed winged fancies—so beautiful and vivid that I was wholly unconscious of my existence as a man.

"And when I awakened, I lay there wondering: Am I a man who dreamed I was a butterfly, or am I a butterfly who dreams he is a man?"

### The Devil's Secret*
(Hindu)

A Hindu who professed to be faithful fulfilled certain sacred rites by giving away some of his livestock. But being both greedy and cunning, he gave away only such as were old or barren and lame.

The Hindu's son cried, "Father, can you not give to Brahman that which you truly treasure?"

His father replied angrily, "Thee I give to the devil."

Heavy of heart, the boy journeyed to the nether world, where the Prince of Darkness asked him, "Why have you come here?"

---

* This story is adapted from a very long philosophical chapter in the *Upanishads*. The *Upanishads,* written in Sanskrit, are a compilation of sayings, insights, visions, without continuity or narrative connection. No one knows how many *Upanishads* there were originally; 108 have been preserved. Each ranges from several hundred to several thousand words. No one knows who wrote them. They are considered the work of saints and seers, and form one of the basic texts of Hindu mysticism.

"To fulfill my father's word."

Moved by this answer, the Devil said, "That is worthy of reverence. Ask me therefore three wishes and they shall be granted."

The boy took thought and said, "Persuade my father to take me back into his heart."

"Done. What is your second wish?"

"Teach me the fire sacrifice that leads to heaven, where none know fear," said the boy.

The Lord of Darkness taught the boy the fire sacrifice. "Now, what is your last wish?"

The boy thought carefully. "When a man's breath ceases," he said, "some say he is dead and some say he has but passed into another life. My last wish, oh Lord of Hell, is to know which is true."

The Devil turned away. "Do not ask this of me. Ask for horses decked in silver or elephants caparisoned in gold. Ask for celestial maidens more beautiful than any mortal has ever seen. Ask for—"

"No, no," the boy cried, "those things do not endure. I ask no other third wish but this: to know the secret of life and death."

And the Prince of Darkness replied, "The fool does not believe in a hereafter; he ends in my domain. But the wise man obeys his mind, not his senses; and his mind obeys the Self. The Self is the lord of time. To be wise, cultivate the Self."

"But what happens to the Self when one dies?" asked the boy.

"The Self prevails, even in death. The Self is Brahman. He who finds the Self is immortal."

"But where can one find this immortal Self?" the boy persisted.

"Only in the heart," said the Prince of Darkness, "only through meditation. As one draws the pith from a reed, so can the seeker of truth separate Self from body. To realize the Self is to find life everlasting."

And so the boy, having learned the Devil's secret, departed

from the kingdom of darkness and found Brahman and became immortal.

## The Mustard Seed
### (Buddhist)

A young woman, having lost her first-born, was so beset with grief that she wandered through the streets, pleading for some magic medicine to restore life to her child. Some turned away from her in pity; some mocked her and called her mad; none could find words to console her.

But a wise man, noting her despair, said, "There is only one in all the world who can perform this miracle. He is the Perfect One, and resides at the top of the mountain. Go to him, and ask."

The young woman went up to the top of the mountain and stood before the Perfect One and beseeched him: "O Buddha, give life back to my child."

And Buddha said, "Go down into the city, and go from house to house, and bring to me a mustard seed from a house in which no one has ever died."

The young woman's heart was high as she hurried down the mountain and into the city. At the first house, she said, "The Buddha bids me fetch a mustard seed from a house which has never known death."

"In this house many have died," they told her.

So she went to the next house, and asked again.

"It is impossible to count the number who have died here," she was told.

She went to a third house and a fourth and a fifth, on and on through the city, and she could not find a single house which death had not at some time visited.

So the grief-stricken young woman returned to the top of the mountain.

"Have you brought the mustard seed?" the Buddha asked.

"No," she said, "nor do I seek it any more.... My grief has made me blind. I thought that only I had suffered at the hands of death."

"Then why have you returned?" the Perfect One inquired.
"To ask you to teach me the truth," she humbly said.
And this is what the Buddha told her:

> "In all the world of man
> And all the world of gods
> This alone is The Law:
> All things are impermanent."

# 17

## EVELYN WAUGH: A Memoir

**E**velyn Waugh once tossed off a wry observation about "the futility of contemporary esteem." Since the publication of his astonishing diaries, one must conclude that Mr. Waugh, the finest satirist of his generation, also scoffed at posthumous approval.

The diaries are devastating. They reveal Waugh to have been eccentric, vain, merciless, an egregious snob, as rude as he was gifted. He chortled over his own maliciousness. He spread shameless gossip without a twinge of guilt. He reveled in petty rancors without a shred of propriety. Perhaps it was his prolonged boozing that explains his hair-raising tales of famous friends: their crazy foibles, inflated egos, sexual hang-ups, sadistic pranks, whoring and treachery and cowardice.

I winced as I read the diaries: I cannot imagine any reasonably decent reader who would not. One of England's leading men of letters, lunching with a group of us at the Savile Club, listened to the heated discussion of Waugh's journals (which were appearing, in purple extracts, in the *Observer*) and finally remarked: "Whatever else one may say about Waugh's talent, which was stupendous, one must use a quaint, now unfashionable, word to describe him as a person: He was an unmitigated cad."

Later that day, I looked up an astonishing passage I had read years ago in Waugh's *A Little Learning: An Autobiography:*

> So little did I follow the news that at the beginning of one term I blithely greeted a man in Balliol with what seemed a pleasantry: "I suppose all your sisters were raped during the vac (vacation)?" To which the sad and candid answer was simply, "Yes." He came from Smyrna.

Waugh's outlandish "pleasantry" reveals, of course, one of his periodic, desperate efforts to be conventional, to make emotional contact with others, to be friendly even to the bores, rotters and fools with whom he consorted. The episode also illustrates his hopeless insensitivity to the sensibilities of others.

Waugh was an altogether original writer, an artist with a mordant eye, an elegant style, a vitriolic wit, a matchless facility for bitchy comment, and a riotous felicity in dissecting characters. Who can ever forget the Countess of Circumference, or little Lord Tangent, or the formidable dowager Metroland?

He wrote exquisite passages of description (*Brideshead Revisited*), incomparable farce (the schoolboys' race in *Decline and Fall,* which ends with a schoolmaster shooting a contestant). He had a marvelous sense of the macabre (the story of the man who loved Dickens) that ranged from journalism (*Scoop*) to London's corybants (*Vile Bodies*) to Hollywood's hallowed cemetery, Forest Lawn (anathematized in *The Loved One*).

Alexander Woolcott, whose name is probably as unfamiliar to Americans under forty as is Herophilus (c. 300 B.C., who anticipated Harvey on the circulation of the blood), once described Waugh's dazzling mockery in these words: "His style has the desperate jauntiness of an orchestra fiddling away for dear life on a sinking ship."

I doubt whether any professional writer or critic will quarrel with the judgment that Waugh was a genius. But he was a man obsessed, tormented by ungovernable terrors.

I confess my admiration for Waugh's writings so that you will not misinterpret what follows: the story of my meeting Mr. Waugh.

My wife and I were spending the summer in London. One day, reading the book section of the morning paper, I sat up in astonishment: there was the name of a book I had written, and a "Review by Evelyn Waugh." I raced through the review, of course, my spine prickling in anticipation of the lacquer-and-acid that was Waugh's trademark. But it was a singularly warm, generous, flattering review.

I had scarcely finished blushing and preening when Victor Gollancz, my publisher, rang me up. In considerable excitement he told me that Waugh, entirely on his own, had written the newspaper to ask if they would like him to review my book. "Waugh *never* does that!" said Gollancz. "He very rarely agrees to review any books."

My wife urged me to write Waugh and invite him to tea. I doubted the wisdom of this, not only because of Waugh's notorious abrasiveness and unpredictability but because it would seem to be apple-polishing.

My wife prevailed.

So I wrote Mr. Waugh a cheerful note, expressing my admiration for his work and inviting him to drop by, at his convenience, for tea or drinks.

I received a swift answer, on a postcard headed "Combe Fleury, Mr. Taunton." The message consisted of three lines:

DEAR L. R.—
   Alas, impossible.
                    E.W.

I was crushed.

My wife was furious. She accused Waugh of unforgivable curtness.

I reminded her that I had not wanted to write him.

She said the man was illegitimate.

I said that my letter was the sort of thing which, in England, just is "not done."

After wrestling with my just resentment and fuming ego, I found a postcard and restored my self-esteem by penning three lines of my own:

DEAR E. W.—
  Quite.
    L.R.

To my surprise, I received a prompt answer by letter, not postcard. The letter was entirely charming. If I would be good enough to forgive him his too-hasty reply, if we would permit him and his wife to come by for tea the following Wednesday, when they would be in London...he had the deepest regard for my works...was a staunch fan...*yearned* to meet me... etc., etc. No apology could have been more gracious.

And so the Evelyn Waughs came to our flat in Whitehall Court, a lovely flat that overlooked the Thames and vibrated in anticipation of its illustrious visitor....

He might have stepped out of Trollope. He was pudgy, moon-faced, pink-cheeked, his skin very clear and shiny, a roly-poly figure in a countryman's heavy tweed suit and waistcoat. It was his eyes that arrested me: small, set far apart in that fair, moony globe, intensely blue; and they glittered. Those eyes glittered from the moment Waugh came in until the moment he left. Their glittering, indeed, bore no relation to his conversation.

He looked like a cherub—a satanic cherub, if you will forgive the oxymoron. He was amiable, impish, vaguely sardonic. He could have been typecast in Hollywood as a pubkeeper. ("Lucifer's Lollipop" was the pub name that ran through my head.)

I suppose that when we meet a famous man, we automatically try to match his appearance with his work. When I first met Robert Maynard Hutchins, I smiled, remembering his "I get all my physical exercise by walking in the funeral cortege of my athletic friends." When I met Bertrand Russell, I could not help recalling his "It is said that man is a rational animal: all my life I have been searching for evidence to support this." When I met Harry Stack Sullivan, I chuckled inwardly at the recollection of his expert psychiatric corker: "The conscience is that part of the personality that dissolves in alcohol."

The line that leaped into my mind when I beheld Evelyn Waugh was from *Decline and Fall:* "'This is my daughter,' said the Bishop with some disgust." It still strikes me as one of the most devastating lines in English.

Mrs. Waugh was pretty, pleasant, an adoring mate. She sat very close to Waugh (who rarely unfolded his hands over his ample paunch). She beamed upon his every word. His every word... well, I trust you will believe what those words were. Here is the gist of our conversation:

ROSTEN: I'm so glad to meet you, after years of reading your——

WAUGH: Why do you wear a double-breasted blazer?

ROSTEN: I beg your pardon?

WAUGH: Is that what they're wearing in the benighted States? (indicating my jacket) *Double-breasted* blazers?

ROSTEN: Y-yes. I bought it in New York. Mr. Waugh, how did you come to write——

WAUGH: (to Mrs. Waugh): Did you hear that? Mr. Rosten bought that *double-breasted* blazer in New York.

MRS. WAUGH: Yes, dear.

ROSTEN: Mr. Waugh, I've always wondered——

WAUGH: What do you call those shoes?

ROSTEN (noticing his own shoes): Uh—they're moccasins—I mean, the U-shaped stitching, on top, is modeled after moccasins.... Did you write——

WAUGH: *Indian* moccasins?

ROSTEN: Yes. When I read your *Put Out More Flags*——

WAUGH: Extraordinary. (To Mrs. Waugh) Do notice Mr. Rosten's shoes. They're moccasins.

MRS. WAUGH: How interesting.

ROSTEN: Was your character in——

WAUGH: *Must* they have such heavy soles?

ROSTEN (noticing soles): I suppose so.... In *Vile Bodies*——

WAUGH: Do you find them comfortable?

ROSTEN: Oh, very. That's why I wear them.

WAUGH: (transfixing me with a glitter): I suppose they are a form of foot-gear described by James Fenimore Cooper....

ROSTEN (gulping): I suppose so.

WAUGH: I should hope so.

Following an agonizing silence my wife poured tea and produced bright small talk. She ran dry.

Waugh said nothing. Mrs. Waugh beamed. I swallowed hard:

ROSTEN: I really must tell you how much I admire your work. When I read *Decline and Fall*, at college——

WAUGH: Are you that young?

ROSTEN: What? Oh.... As for *A Handful of Dust...*! Were you ever in South America?

WAUGH: Mmh.

ROSTEN: How did you happen to get there?

WAUGH: Ship.

ROSTEN (gulping): And to Guiana?

WAUGH: Walked.

After a pause, I noticed Waugh studying my wife's legs. My wife happens to have very shapely legs, but I had never seen an Englishman stare at them so persistently. Mr. Waugh seemed incapable of tearing his eyes away from my mate's gams.

My wife has been known to enlarge decorum on three continents by being absolutely frank, softening her candor with the emollient of amusement.

"Mr. Waugh," she smiled fetchingly, "do I have a run in my stocking, or are you admiring my legs?"

Waugh raised his eyes, enchanted. "The latter. May I say that you do have beautiful legs?"

"Thank you. They're my best feature."

Waugh grinned. To his wife, he said, "*Have* you noticed Mrs. Rosten's legs?"

"Oh, yes, Evelyn. You have *such* lovely legs, Mrs. Rosten."

It all seems vaguely unreal today. Waugh seemed perfectly content to sit there, a florid Humpty Dumpty plumped on a too-small chair, those blue, blue eyes glittering at me, his pixie eyebrows executing a silent dialogue—not with me, but with whatever satirical selves bubbled within him.

He almost never responded directly to anything my wife or I asked, but peppered me with unsettling questions. I could not tell whether he was bored or irritated, mocking me or himself, loathing the *mise-en-scène*, or parodying the institution of tea. When in doubt, he would shoot another admiring look at my loved one's legs, or an amused look at either my blazer or my shoes. They seemed to hypnotize him. . . . I thought the meeting a disaster.

After the Waughs had left, my wife said she was sure that Waugh was agonizingly shy. I was bewildered; never before had I encountered someone so difficult to talk to and so determined to make it more difficult.

Perhaps Waugh, whenever he first met someone, employed the one-upmanship of unexpected and unnerving questions—one after another—either to throw the stranger for a loop or to ward off the possibility of questions one might want to ask him.

Several weeks later, in New York, I received a delightful, warm note from Waugh, out of the blue, about an article I had published on Copernicus: "How I envy you . . . your versatility. You must have the devil in you."

I replied as undiabolically as I could.

He answered in a charming note, mentioning, not as casually as he tried to seem, *The Ordeal of Gilbert Pinfold:* "You may find it of interest.—E. W."

I got the book at once, of course, and read it in one sitting. It was harrowing. It is the story of a man having a nervous breakdown.

Recently, a tutor at Oxford was asked whether he had ever known Evelyn Waugh. "Oh, yes," was the reply, "he was a friend. At one party, he bit me on the ankle."

# 18

## HITLER'S JAW WAS IN HER HANDBAG

**I** am always surprised that other people are not surprised by what surprises me. It may be that my genes simply contain a larger number of surprisable chromosomes than the average Caucasian male with an I.Q. of 43.

Let me illustrate with the story of Adolf Hitler's death. My inordinate surprise is not about that—but about the astonishing lack of impact the following tale registered among even the keenest newshawks in newspaperdom.

Whenever a tabloid is short of sensational copy, or some kook in Rio wants to make the front page, up pops the story that Adolf Hitler is still alive. You can pump life into any party by announcing, "*Hitler was seen this morning in Caracas!*" Or Cairo. Or Tokyo. (But not Tel Aviv.) You can have him spotted *sans* his stubby moustache, or with his hair dyed red, or with a patch over one eye. You can even have him in drag. No matter: People will believe you.

I was reminded of the Hitler-is-alive syndrome when I ran across a London journal's comment on a magazine article in *Znamy,* a Russian magazine, by one Elena Rzhevskaya—a memoir so startling that I cancelled all my appointments and proceeded to read everything I could lay my hands on about Hitler's death. Comrade Rzhevskaya's testimony makes an historic surprise finish to the whole astonishing story.

Hitler's demise was meticulously reconstructed by Prof. H. R. Trevor-Roper in *The Last Days of Hitler.* The Oxford historian, immediately after the war in Europe ended, went to Berlin and used German documents, diaries, intelligence reports—plus interviews with over forty Germans (Hitler's colleagues, officers, secretaries, servants), many of whom had participated in the final hours in a huge bunker under the Chancellery. That redoubt contained a complete communications center, servants' quarters, kitchen, first-aid room, sleeping cubicles for Hitler's doctors (Stumfegger and a certified quack named Morell), and a "suite" for *Der Führer* and Eva Braun, his long-time mistress.

On April 29, 1945, with Russian artillery bombing hell out of Berlin, and with Russian tanks in the Potsdamer Platz, Hitler had his favorite dog poisoned, gave poison ampules to two female secretaries and, at long last, in the underground fastness, married Eva Braun.

On April 30, the Hitlers bade farewell to Goebbels, Martin Bormann (Hitler's schemer-wheedler right-hand man), and to thirteen others, then returned to their quarters in the bunker. At 3:30, a shot was heard. The bodies of Hitler and Eva were found: He had put a bullet through his mouth; she had taken poison.

Their bodies were carried out, up the stairs, and out of an emergency exit—into the garden of the Foreign Office next door. Russian artillery shells were falling all over the place. Gasoline was poured over the two corpses; a rag was lighted and thrown on the bodies, and flames whooshed up. The last loyal watchers gave the Nazi salute. Hitler burned. . . .

All these facts are documented by Trevor-Roper, and by Alan Bullock (*Hitler: A Study in Tyranny*), and by William L. Shirer (*The Rise and Fall of the Third Reich*).

Berlin surrendered on May 2. An official commission of Russian Army doctors conducted a postmortem on the bodies found in the garden. We know that the doctors officially confirmed Hitler's death. *But for eighteen years, the Russians never said so.*

Now, I happened to be in Berlin in September of 1945, staying with General James Gavin. I visited the spot where Hitler and Eva had been incinerated. Sorrow was *not* among my emotions.

No one I met in Berlin—American, British, French or Dutch; soldier, diplomat or intelligence officer, many of whom were in daily contact with the Russians—voiced even a smidgeon of doubt that Adolf Hitler was dead.

I don't want to give you the impression that I made any sort of investigation. I did not. I mention the universal acceptance of Hitler's death because, after the Russians took Berlin, Marshal Georgi Zhukov, commanding the Soviet forces, had told the United Press: "We have found no body definitely identifiable as Hitler's. For all we know, he may be in Spain, or Argentina...."

That started the rumors, all around the globe, that have not died to this day.

Behind all the later *misterioso* concerning Hitler's death, one question loomed large: *Where was Hitler's body?* The question became important for legal reasons—because German and Austrian courts had to decide how to dispose of his assets.

And here my search for Hitler's body, metaphorically speaking, turned up some startling nuggets:

(1) In 1952, the Russians released a film (*The Fall of Berlin*), which accepted the death of Hitler and Eva Braun—without further explanation of any sort.

(2) Fritz Echtmann, identified as "Hitler's former dentist," was released from a prison in Soviet Russia and testified, in an Austrian court, that in Berlin, in May, 1945, the Russians had shown him dentures and a lower jawbone that he had easily and definitely identified as Hitler's! The Austrian court officially declared Adolf Hitler dead....

But the Russians preserved their stony, sulky silence.

(3) In October, 1955, Hitler's valet, Heinz Linge, who had

been in the bunker, returned from a Russian prison camp. Hitler, he said, had shot himself in the mouth. Eva had swallowed poison. Linge himself had carried Hitler's body into the garden. Otto Guensche, an SS man, carried Eva. Both bodies "were doused" with gasoline and set on fire.

Linge said he had reported all this to the Russians nine years earlier.

(4) In 1955, Hans Bauer, Hitler's personal pilot, was released from imprisonment in Russia. He told a group of newsmen how Hitler had said good-bye to him in the bunker "and shot himself."

(5) On March 4, 1959, a British television program showed Hitler's chauffeur, Erich Kempka, saying: "These two bodies (Hitler and Eva) were placed side by side in the garden. I had placed on me the difficult moral duty of pouring petrol on them —and setting fire to them."

(6) In 1960, for the first time, the Russian gates of silence opened—slightly and oddly. The *Kazakhstan Pravda* printed three historic photographs—including one of the dead Hitler, in the garden of the Foreign Office. This was the first picture of Hitler's corpse ever made public.

Ilya Yakovievich Sianov, leader of the Russian detachment that had entered the bunker, was now quoted: "This is a picture of Hitler's corpse.... the hysterical maniac had shot himself at the very last moment. I saw his body. (He) lay there with a hole in his forehead. His servants ... had *no time to burn Hitler's body as he had ordered them to do* [my italics]. Cans filled with gasoline were standing next to his body."

This was the first story to come out of Russia confirming Hitler's death, so far as I know, and the first to deny that Hitler's body had been burned by members of his entourage.

No more news followed from Kazakhstan—or anywhere else in Soviet Russia.

(7) And then—a bonanza. In 1963, Marshal Vasili Sokolovsky, Soviet chief of operations at the Battle of Berlin, told Cornelius Ryan, who was working on his remarkable book, *The*

*Last Battle,* that the Russians, after all, *had* found Hitler's charred body in the garden—but had not made that fact public. Sokolovsky also revealed that the Russians had found Hitler's will. He said no more.

But others did.

(8) Marshal Vasili Chiukov and General B. S. Telpuchovskii told Cornelius Ryan that Hitler's body had been found—and it had been burned! A bullet had blown in the right temple—and knocked out some of Hitler's teeth.

(9) Ryan says that after Berlin fell, Russian experts "found Hitler's body almost immediately (!)... buried under a thin layer of earth." Hitler's teeth "had been knocked out of the head and were lying near it."

Marshal Sokolovsky had promptly ordered a dental check. The Russians located two dental "technicians" in Berlin who had worked for Hitler's dentist: Fritz Echtmann (note!) and Käthe Heusermann. The Russians asked Echtmann to sketch Hitler's teeth from memory.

Echtmann's sketches agreed in every detail with the actual jaw, teeth and dental work, which he was then shown.

Käthe Heusermann, picked up later, was shown the jaw, teeth and dental work, and she asserted that they were undoubtedly Hitler's.

And now, as climax to this bizarre charade, I give you the London report I read of the Russian magazine article by Elena Rzhevskaya. She was an interpreter attached to Russian Army Headquarters and was in Berlin when the city fell. She says that Russian Army doctors conducted a post-mortem on Hitler's body, and then *they gave the jaw and teeth to her* and an army officer—ordering them to find Hitler's dentist and clinch the identification.

Comrade Rzhevskaya placed Hitler's jaw in her handbag and, with the army officers, set forth across the demolished city on their macabre treasure hunt.

They could not find Hitler's dentist, but they did track down Käthe Heusermann—who led them back to the bunker and into a little dental office. There she found and produced—the X-rays of Hitler's mouth! The X-rays checked in every respect with the jaw in Elena Rzhevskaya's handbag.

Comrade Rzhevskaya ends her memoir crisply:

> Hitler's teeth, the infallible proof of his death, and all the pertinent documents *were sent to Moscow* [my italics].

But the Russian authorities never told any of this to anyone. Where *is* Hitler's body?

Years later, the Russians told Cornelius Ryan they had cremated the charred body (!) of Hitler just outside Berlin. They would not say where. They said they had buried the body of *Der Führer* in an undisclosed place to prevent its becoming a shrine or an inspiration to fanatical Nazis—or their descendants.

So the next time some wiseacre tells you that Hitler was seen yesterday sailing down the Irawaddy in a sampan steered by Martin Bormann, put him down with a superior smile. Better yet, brandish Elena Rzhavskaya's memoir in his face. It's entitled *Berlinskie Stranitsy,* from the magazine *Znamy No. 5.* It costs 55 kopecks. I suspect you'd have a hard time finding a copy.

*Postscript*

Proof of Hitler's death, and in such dramatic form, is surely no run-of-the-mill news item. I published the facts you just read way back in 1967, in *Look* magazine.

Not a single American newspaper or press association, columnist or editorial writer or gossip column (for heaven's sake!) ever mentioned it. So far as I know no American journal to this day has ever told the extraordinary story.

I can't for the life of me tell you why. I guess my startle reflex, or my capacity for surprise, is un-American.

# 19

---

## A LESSON IN POLITICS

**D**uring those historic months when the New Left was demonstrating its love of free speech by denying it to others, its devotion to peace by using violence, its love of Love by monstrous hate of everyone from professors to Presidents, its dedication to democracy by attacking it like Nazis, its thirst for education by wrecking classrooms and burning buildings, its sensitive soul by hurling obscenities distasteful to drunken bums, its superior thinking by mouthing silly slogans drawn from mushy ideologies, its non-conformity by responding like sheep to unstable shepherds or demented demagogues—during those idealistic orgies I conducted a series of interviews which followed the most rigorous standards of Lou Harris, George Gallup and other seasoned takers-of-the-public-pulse. My survey revealed that twenty-eight percent of the students, and only twenty-four percent of the faculties, were nuts.

I have just completed a new survey, and must change these sad figures. This poll embraced a representative sample not of Academe but of the American people at large. After totting up the figures, I spent six days in meditation and four nights in prayer; for it seems that *thirty-two percent* of our population is nuts—and, mind you, this does not even include the inhabitants of New York's City Hall.

Are you crying "Shame!" Are you calling me a cynic, a reactionary, a social scientist? Please don't. Just consider, for example, that call to civic duty we all have drummed into our ears by radio and into our eyes by print and TV: Vote! Do your duty as a citizen! Get out and Vote!

This stirring call is usually followed by worthy words about the sanctity of the franchise, the precious privilege of free men, and the boons of casting a ballot in this land which is my land which I love as much as you do.

Now: Have you ever suspected that the patriotic call to "Vote! Vote! Vote!" rests on the unexamined premise that it doesn't matter whom or what you vote for—just vote? The premise is dangerous and the consequences often disastrous.

I think it matters very much for whom you vote; and I maintain that if you don't know a good deal about whom you are voting for (therefore, whom you are voting against), what he stands for, what his party/program promises to do, what the probable *consequences* of voting X and his party into office will mean, then—I plead—true patriotism should lead you *not to vote*. Moreover, you should run around begging the like-befuddled to follow your patriotic example.

Are you crying "Hair-splitter!" "Word twister!" "Philadelphia lawyer!"?

Please reconsider. My argument is straightforward: If all the citizens who vote carelessly, or in a trance, or because of their friends' political convictions (and biases), or for a party they blindly support come-hell-or-high-water; if all the voters who take neither the time nor the trouble to analyze and agonize over issues and candidates—if all these resolutely prevented themselves from entering election booths, our country would be far, far better off.

Why? Because the fateful decisions which will surely alter

all our lives would be made by those voters who do take the time and trouble to think—to think long, tough, and hard—before casting that portentous ballot. Thinking is hard work; thinking long, tough, and hard is exhausting.

So the good folk who parrot "Vote! Vote!" are, without realizing it, doing a dreadful disservice to the public good. Since they urge people to vote without thinking, they give as much weight to stupidity as they do to intelligence. They urge the ignorant to cancel out the less-ignorant. They prompt the indecent to be as influential as the decent. They tip the scales in favor of the organized and obedient, at the expense of the unorganized and free-minded.

Are you now accusing me of snobbery, "elitism," intellectualism? Please don't. Democracy does not deny human differences, different preferences, and different values. Indeed, it assumes that each mortal soul is right in "doing your own thing." (How graceless a phrase, when so many better ones abound: even the clichéd "Be your own self" should make its usurper blush.) Democracy assumes that each man or woman will decide, without state pressure or deception, whom to vote for, what to vote for, and when to exercise the right not to vote at all. (Those behind the Iron Curtain, in Red China, or in "progressive" Cuba who do not vote are punished for their defection from the sacred principles of liberated slavery—or, if you prefer, enslaved liberation.)

I think enough of the deeper good sense of those who evangelize Voting to predict that if they will but think of the consequences of what they preach, they will recognize how inane and dangerous is a course of action that propels dimwits, goons, fanatics, book-censors, cross-burners, psychopaths, and yahoos into those curtained booths where the state of freedom, no less than "free" goodies from city, state or Congress, is periodically affected.

Let me illustrate this sermon with a memorable event that occurred on November 10, 1966, in Miami, Dade County, Florida. On that day a Mr. Charles P. English, Republican candidate for a place on the county school board, received 80,644 votes.

Mr. English, it happened, was incarcerated in the Kalamazoo (Michigan) State Hospital at the time the election was being held and while 80,644 Floridians were voting for him. Mr. English had been in a mental institution for seven months before November 10, 1966. He had been escorted to benevolent confinement after trying to enter the office of Governor George P. Romney, which is no legal offense, except that Mr. English was carrying a loaded pistol in his briefcase whilst so doing. (The laws are perfectly clear in stating that it is illegal to enter Governor Romney's office with a loaded firearm in your briefcase and unfriendly intentions in your mind.)

How on earth did Mr. English get his name on the ballot? The story as reported in *The New York Times* (an item I clipped and framed in silver) states that Mr. English had simply paid the "qualifying fee" which made him, a registered voter, eligible to run for public office.

The story grows curiouser. The Republican Committee of Dade County tried its very best to remove Mr. English's name from the list of Republican candidates. They failed. And so it was that ritualistic Republicans, long exhorted to "Vote! Vote! Vote!", fulfilled their solemn civic duty by trudging to the election premises. A certified inmate in Michigan received 80,644 votes from the ambulatory outmates of Dade County. Fortunately, Mr. English's Democratic opponent received 159,725 votes.

I say "fortunately" not because I wish to cast aspersions on Republicans. Why, I know otherwise-sane Democrats who voted for Henry Wallace in 1948—or, more recently, for a Congressman, beholden to the donkey banner, whose marbles have long since left considerable space in his never-crowded cerebellum. I even have heard that many a Democrat believed that Eugene McCarthy would make a good President of the United States— a notion dispelled from their affections by the Senator's behavior after the New Hampshire primary. *My* skepticism was early engendered by friends in the Senate and the Washington press corps, and was thoroughly fortified by the later testimony of some of Gene McCarthy's most dedicated and intelligent young disciples.

Nor, I hasten to anticipate you, am I a Republican. I still suffer from memories of Warren Gamaliel Harding; or Herbert Hoover (a man of commanding intelligence, if you read his book on the problems of power and governing, but a man pathetically miscast as a politico); or Dwight D. Eisenhower (whom I liked immensely—and voted against), whose irrelevant, intrusive, rampaging virtue during the Suez take-over by England, France, and Israel converted a boon for Middle Eastern stability into the catastrophic *status quo ante.*

If you are wondering, as you must be, what my political affiliation *is,* I am panting to tell you. I am a liberal, independent, who yearningly hopes that our economists could agree on an economic program, and our foreign-affairs experts on such things as SALT or Helsinki.

I am a saddened citizen who has been compelled to see that the best-meaning social planners, whether Democrat, Republican, Demo-Republicans or Republico-Democrats (no need to *point,* Suzie), have inflicted social and economic disasters on our cities, our housing, our slums, our schools, our race relations, our tax blood, and our precious individual freedom.

They have done so not because they are stupid or malevolent or ill-informed. They have done so because they assumed that humane intentions will produce laudable results. They have made unexamined pre-judgments, used shaky sociology, followed faulty economics, and displayed a guilt-ridden reluctance to study the facts—that is, the actual consequences of well-intentioned programs. It is for this reason that very *good* men can do as much harm to the body politic as bad men can. And reformers never seem to consider the possibility that things can be made worse....

They have not learned how very, very complex human organization is; how much more complex and perverse welfare programs become the moment they leave the blueprints and statistical tables; how often efforts to help the old, the young, the blacks, the poor, turn out (in overt or hidden forms) to hurt them; how often price-and-wage ceilings become price-and-wage floors; how minimum-wage laws mock their legislators by increasing disemployment among the least-skilled and the lowest paid—and by creating non-employment among the young (especially blacks) who desperately need jobs and training-on-the-job, and when barred from working (by punitive wage fences), too often are driven to use dope, then push it.

The most deeply entrenched and dangerous idea in both government and the populace is that any political problem can be solved (some simply cannot be), any social inequity abolished (stupidity, cruelty, chicanery, congenital criminality cannot be), any human ailments healed (billions of dollars have not slain the common cold) and all individual grievances satisfied. A corollary to the myths so skimpily sketched above is the notion that human and social problems can be resolved swiftly. And as the crowning folly, I give you the well-documented fact that a whopping number of Democrats and Republicans have not learned that appropriating *money* will not solve some problems at all, or as fast as would objective, hard-nosed efforts to analyze them, understand them, seek their causes (the causes are nearly all numerous, and rarely simple), experiment with small-scale alternative efforts designed to diminish (much less end) them—*before* floods of cash are released (and your taxes increased) in fervent but foredoomed generosity.

Draw up your own balance-sheet correlating "Monies Appropriated" (to correct the following) with "Present Conditions": poor farmers, urban crime, inflation, postal service, juvenile delinquency, city rejuvenation, Project Headstart, the robbery rate, the rape rate, dope addiction, muggings, stabbings, stompings, etc.

I ask you, *pro bono publico,* only to ponder my lamentations. And if you scoff that my opening estimate of the proportion of lunatics in our fair, tormented land is cockeyed, consider one final bit of advice: look around.

H. L. Mencken, the best political satirist we have yet turned out, used to describe the United States fondly as "a mob of serfs" whose average intelligence is so abysmal that any man who has read fifty books and does not believe in ghosts is sure to be a howling success. No phase of American life, however mighty or sanctimonious, escaped the merciless fusillade of Mencken's mockery: Church, Home, the Press, Mother Love, Patriotism, the Honest Poor, the Deserving Rich. He lambasted the Courts, the Congress, and the Clergy; he named judges he considered crooked, politicians he considered scoundrels, and reformers he considered frauds. He had the sharpest eye since Mark Twain for the phony, and the clearest and most incorruptible awareness of those iron necessities which constitute freedom.

The best testimonial I know to what we call "the American way" is the fact that Mencken was neither tried for treason nor lynched. I sometimes wonder how he escaped it. Yet there is no real cause for wonder; the secret lies in the miracle of that consensus which is held by all but the un-American: that we defend the rights of those we hate or fear or despise.

The greatest political invention known to the race of man is the idea that men shall be protected in their right to criticize, denounce and oppose the state itself, the police, the powers-that-be; that men shall be free to think what they please, read what they please, say what they please—so long as it is within the realm of legality, and does not incite to violence in circumstances of "clear and present danger."

The entire intricate structure of our freedom rests on two things: a philosophical commitment and a political device. The commitment is this: to separate opinions from crimes, dissent from treason, opposition from heresy, the disturbing from the dangerous. The distinction between ideas and deeds, between what a man says and what he does, is the central article of a democratic faith which tyrants, lunatics and Communists cannot understand: being too weak to tolerate, much less encourage, argument, they punish men for asking questions and slaughter them for raising doubts.

The political device by which democracy perpetuates the

philosophical commitment is this: a built-in way of effecting *change without violence*. Under no other system is it possible to make significant changes in power without killing off some people, disenfranchising others, exiling a few or jailing a good many. (The British, incidentally, can legislate more sweeping changes on shorter notice and with less hullabaloo than we do, since their Parliament is not hobbled by constitutional chains; I often thank God that Congress is.)

We are a people who govern ourselves by rules which describe the ways in which we can even remove our governors. We accept the obligations of a compact which asks us to hold in check the natural human impulse to beat up those we dislike, imprison those we fear, or murder those we hate. And all this works, I think, because of a few crucial ideas which we respect, whether we articulate them or not:

1. Power is power over others, and power over others must always be watched, guarded and circumscribed.

2. No man, no group, no sect, no party ever has a monopoly on truth, virtue and competence.

3. No man, no class, no group, no party is good enough, wise enough *and* sane enough to be entrusted with too much power. For good men are often silly, competent men are often wicked, and even the combination of virtue and ability does not in the slightest way guarantee reason. It is sad but true that good intentions do not necessarily lead to good results, and that purity of heart is not always linked to either skill or sanity, much less both. Human history is a tragedy precisely because too often men have seized, or been permitted to enjoy, the power to do what *they* thought best.

4. Those we like may be wrong; those we hate may be right. The best way to find out what is best, for whom, is to let the ideas and the theories roll out in uninterrupted contest.

5. Freedom dies under dogma; in a free society no person or group or policy can be permitted to exist beyond scrutiny and criticism. When dogma gains enough power to punish those who oppose it, it becomes fanaticism; when dogma is invested with

enough power to suppress opposition, it becomes tyranny. When men are afraid to say what they think—however cock-eyed, however unpopular—freedom has been corrupted by fear.

6. The only thing worse than a too-powerful minority is a too-powerful majority. Government must protect all minorities against any majority—including itself.

7. Every man has a right to opportunity, respect, and fair treatment under law. Justice is a right, not a favor. No man shall be penalized for his name, his parentage, his pigmentation, or his opinions.

8. No man, however disagreeable or dangerous, can be denied a full, free, open trial, on specific charges, for specific acts; and no man shall be judged by the same people who accuse him.

9. It is up to the authorities to prove a man guilty; it is not up to him to prove himself innocent.

10. The purpose of government is so to arrange things that people can privately do what they damn please—so long as it does not harm or menace others.

This is my democratic decalogue. It rests, of course, on the conviction that government must protect men from each other's stupidity, greed and passions.

Since no one knows all the answers to all problems all the time, and since new problems always arise, a democracy must be unremittingly resilient; it must adapt itself to reality without sacrificing its final values. This it does by guaranteeing that changes can be made legally, through political mandate, without force, without trickery, without subversion, without violence.

Plato described democracy as a "charming form of government, full of variety and disorder, dispensing a kind of equality to equals and unequals alike." I cherish both the variety and the disorder.

# 20

---

## THE CIGAR: A Fervent Footnote to History

No one who is not a nicotine addict can know the raging craving of those who love to smoke. From my sixteenth year on, I devoured at least one pack of cigarettes a day. Now, having kicked the habit, I live in a state of superior virtue.

But how well I know the power of the passion for tobacco (the most priceless, it turned out, of all the things Columbus found in the New World), and how deeply I feel for those in bondage to the sweet evil. Like Robin Shlemiel.

It happened in Washington during World War II. Robin was a clean-cut, patriotic helot in the State Department. His first name is not really Robin, and his last name is certainly not Shlemiel (he is more of a Stuyvesant than a Shlemiel); but I want to spare him embarrassment should his children happen to read these words.

Robin, a Princeton graduate, entered the State Department in a lowly capacity, but by demonstrating exceptional probity, vision and correct spelling, he raced up the spatsy ladder to become a speech-writer for our august Secretary of State.

Now it came to pass (a phrase that usually precedes bad news) that the Secretary of State was scheduled to deliver an important speech at a Monday night dinner for 800 dignitaries. And Robin was obliged to blend a dozen departmental drafts of that speech into one historic oration.

How Robin worked on that fateful text over the weekend! He told his wife, Hester, how important was the assignment on which he was working. He deafened his ears to the importunings of his children, and resolutely bolted the door of his study. There—on a desk, sills, cabinets, floor—Robin spread out all the working drafts and policy guidelines and Top Secret alarums from G-2, B.E.W., GRUNT, GROAN, and KRECHTZ.* Had you seen Robin's study at a time like this, you would know what Sherman meant when he said, "War is hell."

By 10:00 P.M. on the fateful Sunday night, Robin Shlemiel headed into the Final Draft. He reached for a cigarette.... The pack was empty.

Robin cursed. He opened a desk drawer, then another and another. No cigarettes. He stormed into the living room and ran through the teak-boxes and the glass coffin where Hester always kept cigarettes. He found not one fag.

So he collected all the butts in the ashtrays and lighted one after another greedily, singeing his fine, patrician nose in the service of his country—and wrote on. He puffed out all the butts he could find, and by 10:45 not a smidgeon of a stub remained.

So Robin scoured the kitchen, and disemboweled two cabinets in vain. He ran upstairs and rummaged through every closet— frisking every pocket in his coats, suits, robes, pajamas. He hopped around like a sex-starved rabbit, opening bon-bon boxes and Wedgwood jars and containers for buttons and needles.

---

* G-2 (Army intelligence), B.E.W. (Board of Economic Warfare), GRUNT (General Representatives of Underdeveloped Nations' Trade), GROAN (General Report on Overall Ailments of Nations), and KRECHTZ (the most active—and certainly the most eloquent—activity in Washington).

By this time Hester was wide awake. When Robin told her about his Armageddon, they frantically searched together. They searched high, they searched low, they even searched each other. They probed under couch cushions, wiggled under sofas, sifted through waste baskets. They even burst into the garage to savage the car seats and glove compartment. Alas and alack, not a single cigarette humanized the entire house ("goddamn house" is actually what Robin called it) or garage ("X!#!6!" is how Robin described it).

You may be wondering why Robin did not slake his raging nicotiniphilia by hopping into his car and zipping over to the corner drugstore or friendly supermarket. And if you *are*, it shows how ignorant you are of the mores which strait-jacketed our nation's capital. Drugstores in that quasi-Southern metropolis closed around 9 o'clock, when I was doing time there—and still may shut down by 10, for all I know.

By 11:36, Robin had sunk into a Queen Anne chair, babbling, and Hester was wringing her Hawthorne hands.

"Oh ——!" shouted Robin, taking the name of the Lord in vain. "Why, *our whole* postwar policy may depend upon this speech, and—"

It was at this point that Robin's glazing eyes unglazed—for they had fallen upon The Cigar. A vulpine gloat oozed across his features. ...

The Cigar rested inside a small, sealed glass case, beautifully edged in silver, which occupied the place of honor in the center of the mantel on the marble fireplace. The Cigar had adorned— nay, had sanctified—every mantelpiece in every abode Robin and Hester had occupied from the day they were married. The Cigar and its case ranked as a family heirloom—Hester's family, that is. An elegantly inscribed silver plate, screwed with tiny silver screws into the mahogany base of the case, read:

This Cigar
Was Presented To
Sgt. Martin Willoughby
of the 83rd Infantry
by
LT. GEN. ULYSSES S. GRANT
During the Parade up Fifth Avenue in
New York City, May, 1866

Robin's eyes glittered as he rose.

"No! No!" Hester flung her body between the husband she loved and The Cigar she had inherited.

"It's not for *me*...." Robin murmured.

"Grandfather Willoughby put that cigar in his *will!*" pleaded Hester.

"I know." Robin leered. "But this is a *national emergency!*"

"My grandfather broke ranks while his regiment was parading up Fifth Avenue because he was so overcome with emotion when he beheld Ulysses S. Grant in the front row of the reviewing stand!"

"Yes, dear." Robin was looking around for a stout destructive object.

"And he *crawled* up that reviewing stand to cry, 'General Grant, I served under you at Shiloh!' "

"Quite so, darling...."

"And Ulysses S. Grant *in person*—" Hester's eyes were flashing fire now "—leaned down and extended his hand and said, 'Mighty proud to know you, son!'—and General Grant *handed Grandfather Willoughby that cigar!!*"

"How fortunate." Robin smiled, unlacing a shoe.

"No! I forbid it!" cried Hester.

"Think!" thundered Robin. "If Grandfather Willoughby was here, right now, in this very room, knowing *why* I want to do such a dastardly thing as to break that case and take that immortal cigar and light it up and smoke it so that *I can do my duty to our country*—"

"No..." whimpered Hester.

"—making it possible for the Secretary of State to make a critical wartime speech—"

Hester Lou was sniveling incoherently.

"—I ask you, in all candor and honesty," slashed Robin, "what do you think that peerless patriot, Martin Willoughby of the 83rd Infantry, would say?...Don't blubber, Hester. Be brave. Be honest. What do you think—what do you *know*, in your heart of hearts, Grandpa Martin Willoughby would say?!"

Moaned Hester, "He would say, 'Your country calls, son. Nothing should stand between a man and his duty.'...Go on, darling. I can't bear it. I shall avert my eyes....Break the glass!"

Robin looked as noble as Lancelot as he raised his shoe, converting the heel into a hammer, and tap-tap-tapped the glass. It cracked.

Carefully, tenderly, Robin extracted the shards from their silver frame, and he lifted the cigar out with the reverence it merited, and he lovingly savored its aroma (fresh and fragrant, because of the airtight casing), and he struck a match, brought the flame to the tip of the cigar, sucked in three deliriously delicious puffs, exhaled the smoke in a blissful cloud—and the cigar exploded.

The cigar exploded in Robin's face just the way it should have exploded in Martin Willoughby's face, eighty-eight years earlier, just the way Ulysses S. Grant, a notorious prankster, had wanted. Old "Unconditional Surrender" used to pass out trick cigars right and left, for reasons no biographer has been frank enough to explain, and no psychoanalyst brave enough to reveal.

The tale of The Cigar brings a lump to my throat whenever I think of it. It was the longest-delayed practical joke in American history.

The story is absolutely true.

# 21

## THE ENGLISH AND THE JEWS

**C.** P. (Lord) Snow recently began a book review in London's *Financial Times* with these arresting lines:

You are required to answer the following question. Which of these two contemporary artistic experiences causes you greater discomfort, or embarrassment, or shyness? The first is a short prose account of a man's love for his father. The love is open and unrestrained. The father, through the son's eyes, is as decent as a man can be. When he dies, the son, now a middle-aged man, goes swimming so that he can cry unobserved. The second experience is a film, in which the central figure is tortured in such a way that you can watch the limits of torture: and then burned to death.... Which of these two offerings has cost you the most discomfort? The answer is easy. If you are a child of our time (and most of us, whether we like it or not, are) the spectacle of torture will have cost you no discomfort at all. You have gone there in a chase for sensation. You are not perturbed by sensation; it doesn't produce a ripple of emotion.

It is altogether different when, as in the first example, you are faced by direct emotion. Now you become very shy. In fact, you are shocked. A man ought not to love his father; or, if he can't help it, he certainly ought not to say so. Torture is well within the rules of the permissible; emotional display, much less emotional exuberance, is totally outside it. There must be something very wrong with such a man. If he is Jewish (as the author proudly and happily is), you feel he has to be disposed of by the word *schmaltz.*

Lord Snow then turns the tables on the English reader by analyzing the hypocrisy of the first response (to father-love), and the hasty *defense against emotions* (to torture) of the second. Why are the English so uneasy about the direct expression of strong human feeling?

I read this review several times, with more than ordinary interest; not only because the "short prose account of a man's love for his father" was written by me (the book being reviewed was *People I Have Loved, Known or Admired*) but because Lord Snow so strikingly raised a question that has fascinated me since the time when I went to study in London many years ago. I love England beyond measure, and my friends there are close to my affections and values and lifestyle.

And now I think I know some answers to Lord Snow's question: Englishmen prize privacy; Jews prize intimacy. The English dislike displaying their feelings; Jews think feelings are meant to be verbalized. Englishmen understate the serious ("The riot was a bit of a mess") and overstate the trivial ("What a *frightfully* amusing hat!"); Jews tend to inflate what is important ("That will blacken his name for all time!") and pooh-pooh what is not cataclysmic ("Stroke-schmoke, he can still wink with one eye!"). The English repress uneasiness; Jews feed it banquets of nourishment. An Englishman treats a disaster as unfortunate; a Jew thinks a hangnail an injustice. The English are embarrassed by confidences; Jews are let down by "coldness." The English place a premium on the concealment of emotion (in a crisis, John Bull does "fly into a calm"); they voice a deep conviction as if it were a tentative opinion; they are made uncomfortable by a raised voice or a trickled tear; they disapprove of the dogmatic—and all of this puzzles people (besides Jews) who were steeped in other modalities of affect. Where Egypt wails, England blinks. Where Hindu women tear their hair, English women study their nails. An Italian explodes invective; an Englishman sniffs, "Really?" When the Russians thunder, "*Every*one knows....," the English demur, "But I should think that...." Where Americans cry, "It's terrific!" Englishmen concede, "Rather impressive." And where Englishmen murmur, "What a pity," Jews cry, "What a disaster!"

These differences in what anthropologists call "character structure" are crucial to anyone who tries to understand values foreign to his own or to comprehend conduct that departs from his ingrained expectations. Jews may strike Anglo-Saxons as verbose and melodramatic because Jews are early taught (as I was) to feel an *obligation* to respond to the misfortunes of others with visible, audible sympathy—so that no one can possibly fail to recognize the depth and sensitivity of one's compassion. To Jews, emotions are not meant to be nursed in private: they are meant to be dramatized and displayed—so that they can be *shared*. What is sweeter than a tearful or gleeful *shmooz:* a juicy exchange of feelings or frustrations, dreams and experiences? Not to do this, O Albion, is to lack "true feeling," to be blinded by selfish preoccupations, to fail as a *mensh.*

I suppose that whereas a psychiatrist regards "empathy" as feeling for others, a Jew considers empathy heartless if it does not give equal time to himself. It is not that Jews (or Greeks or Arabs) are genetically maudlin and wallow in wailing and hyperbole; they have just been taught that it is healthier to express than repress; that one must help those in stress by echoing their lamentations (which reduces their burden); that to embroider one's own emotions is an obligation to your fellow men—who are entitled to participate in your miseries, no less than your triumphs, as you are in theirs.

The English think "a stiff upper lip" is a sign of courage; Mediterranean people judge a "stiff upper lip" to be *inappropriate* (why should suffering cast doubt on courage?)—since eyes filled with tears and eloquent expressions of consolation can give so much comfort to those, stricken by fate, who have been raised, too, to expect men to be *simpatico*, to act decently, to be *sympatish* conveyors of "feeling-with."

But delicate gradations of tact lie beneath these surfaces of deportment. At a funeral, a Jew is expected to lament and wail and weep; but during *shiva*, the seven days of mourning at home, he comes to pay his respects and offers no greeting at all, for he must be (or at least appear to be) so deeply plunged in grief, so compassionate toward the bereaved, that speech is beyond his powers.

After long, precious immersion in three cultures, accustomed from my crib on to gales of laughter and epiphanies of disaster, I have come to the conclusion that Americans treat "neurotic" as a synonym for "nuts"; that Englishmen think "neurotic" an adjective applicable to foreigners; and that Jews consider "neurotic" a synonym for "human."

# 22

## FAREWELL TO COCKTAILS

**I** went to a snazzy cocktail party the other day. It had five times as many people as any sane doctor would force into a padded cell, more noise than a subway platform at rush hour, Martinis ten times as paralyzing as any drinker should welcome, nauseous teeny-weenies in underbaked rolls—but I'm repeating myself: "cocktail party" is enough to give you the picture.

That silly shivaree is the last of such tribal rites I shall ever attend. It contained, I admit, as *distingué* a mob as you can find outside of Who's Who. It was especially strong on Intellectuals who were renewing their credentials as Seminal Thinkers by using words like *paradigm, parameter, perception,* and *pejorative.*

The "In" words this year all begin with "P." Last year was a "C" year, what with *charisma* and *caucus* crawling around like caterpillars in Connecticut. (Alliteration is a cinch.) Today, "metaphor" is building up such a head of steam that, with "mythic" and "*manqué,*" we are headed for a fat "M" season.

Shortly after I plunged into the yakking crowd of biped cattle, and for no reason except that he is working on a book about it, a professor of theological embroidery accosted me. "How do you

explain the fact," he sternly asked, "that the 'Is God dead?' con-
troversy, which created such a furor in so many circles, has died
away with such— —" I *think* he said "resounding vapidity," but
it may well have been "astounding rapidity."

I glanced into my low-ball glass thoughtfully, which is *de
rigueur* when a member of the Harvard faculty is present, and
replied, "One often ponders the parameters of that paradigm."

"Precisely!" He walked away, beaming.

His place was taken by a buxom siren with a Buster Brown
hair-do (by Sassoon), who bristled, "Was Homer trying to tell
you God can't possibly be a woman?!"

"Who's Homer?"

"Homer *Cooze!*" she retorted. "He was just here, bending your
ear with that pejorative 'Is God Dead?' ploy he uses to— —"

"Who's Cooze?"

"You mean you don't *know?* You haven't *read* 'God lives on
the Third Floor of 23 East 64th Street'?!"

"No. . . . Why does Professor Cooze claim God can't possibly
be a woman?"

"Because the Bible," she sneered, "says 'man and woman
created *He* them!' Have you ever heard such *non*sense?"

"Often."

Her eyes alone would have qualified her for the lead in *The
Godmother.* "Where?"

I couldn't remember where, so I quipped: "Don't blame
God: She's only human."

Slapping her back dislodged the ice cube from her throat.

This action whipped Homer Cooze back to my side. "What
the hell are you doing to my wife?!"

"Your wife?" I echoed. "I didn't know you were harried."

"I'll thank you to keep unpleasant facts out of this! She is a
female chauvinistic pig. Now then, no shilly-shallying! I ask
you bluntly: *Do you or do you not believe in God?!*"

"I have been asked that question before," I rejoined with a
moue. "And I have not the slightest hesitation in giving you a
blunt answer."

"Then why don't you?"

"I'm searching for my amulet.... Your question, if I may re-formulate it, is this: Do I—that is, my palpable congregation of nuclear subuniverses—separated from your nuclear mass by (if we believe Newton) the inverse square of distance—"

"*Well* put," he murmured, "*well* put!"

"—include, in the equation with which I try to find meaning in either an expanding or contracting universe, *neither* of which can escape Heisenberg's principle of indeterminacy or Godel's Law that shows that logic, *by its very construction,* cannot answer certain questions—do I include the variable of a Prime Force or First Mover?"

"Exactly! *Splen*did! Do you?"

"That is a good question," I said, moving on.

The cluster of high, tight-skinned brows I now invaded was discussing an entirely different subject, I was happy to see. They were winging in exceptionally verbose orbit around the question: "Was *The Greening of America* the funniest, phoniest, or sickest book of our day?"

A third congregation of cerebral massagers was huddled in a corner, where they had trapped one of our nation's leading economists. The poor man's eyes were as glazed as doughnuts, because his peers were asking: "How can Professor Milton Samuelson claim that any Wage-Price Controls must be a success that failed, instead of being *either* a failure that succeeded or a *post hoc ergo propter hoc* pitfall based on an econometric model that *leaves a good deal to be desired?*"

"How true!" I cried.

When this group began to extrapolate price spirals from cost-pushes and wage-pulls, to say nothing of consumer vectors, I stumbled over a *non-sequitur* and fell upon the sofa—right next to a mountainous man who was surrounded by fearless exponents of our country's Alienation Syndrome. "But Freud never maintained that foot-fetishists should play squash!" a Radcliffe donness exclaimed.

"*Touché!*" the horizontal pundit gasped.

A flunky asked me if I cared to "freshen up my drink."

"No," I said, "diminish it."

Standing there amidst the bearded and the bra-less who were hop-scotching around the Scotch, I heard a brouhaha bust out about *Art Nouveau* and *Cinéma Vérité* and "Is Gloria Friedan the daughter of Kate Abzug—*metaphorically* speaking, of course?"

The minute I heard "metaphorically" I went home.

# 23

## HOW SPIRO AGNEW WAS CHOSEN

**A**re you still wondering how in the world Richard Nixon ever came to choose Spiro Agnew as his running mate? I'm not. I happen to know the inside story.

One night, a decade ago, as they were dining in the ornate Executive Mansion in Baltimore, Governor Agnew sighed to his lovely wife, "Honey, I'm depressed. I was real happy when I was selling automobile insurance, or supervising that crummy supermarket. I had dreams then, dreams of higher things to come. But now I'm governor of Maryland—*all* of Maryland—and to tell you the truth, the fun just seems to have gone out of things. Anywhere I look, there's no future to this scam. Let's be honest, doll: Where can I go from here?"

"We-el," said Mrs. Agnew." You *might* try for Vice President."

"Shucks, mother," said the Governor, "for an important job like *that,* who'd ever think of a poor Greek boy like me? I'm no nattering nabob, no Fancy Dan of negative nit-picking."

"That's true," gloomed Mrs. Agnew. Then, blurting it out (as great ideas often are), she cried, "Ted! Why not put your name in the yellow pages!"

"Pass the chili sauce," said the Governor, remembering his marriage vows.

Our scenario dissolves to Richard Milhous Nixon's suite at the Hilton Plaza in Miami Beach, on the historic night of August 7, 1968. The Republican convention had just nominated Mr. Nixon as their presidential candidate after a long, hard, dull first ballot.

Now, to his assembled loved ones, cohorts, colleagues and advisers, Mr. Nixon solemnly declared, "I want to make one thing absolutely clear: I haven't the faintest idea of who—or even whom—to choose as my running mate! I mean for Vice President. I've given it oodles of thought, and I'm flat-out stumped. I'm like a quarterback without a running back to pass off to. Without one tight end on the team to lob a pass to. Without a trap play or a receiver for the long bomb.... So let's go around the room, man by man, and give me your frank, honest, open and above-board opinion! Who or whom should I tap for V.P.?. ... Tom."

Governor Dewey said, "Tap Nelson Rockefeller!"

"Or his telephone," said a voice from under the table.

Nominee Nixon made some strangling sounds, but coolly recovered: "Let me make one thing absolutely clear, Tom: I like Nelson just as much as the next fellow" (the next fellow happened to be Barry Goldwater, who never liked Rockefeller inordinately) "but let's face it, team: Nelson looks like a new-car salesman! Those goddamn Democrats will murder a Nixon-Rockefeller slate at the polls, because they'll spread a lot of dirty propaganda that I only chose Rocky in order to snare liberal voters, which would be true.... Ray, who or whom do you recommend?"

Ray Bliss, GOP National Chairman, said, "How about John Lindsay?"

Mr. Nixon's full, strong jaw dropped. "N-no," he said thoughtfully. "Lindsay's too goddamn *tall* for a V.P. He'd be looming all over me all the time.

"I hate loomers," said Ron ("Shorty") Nessen.

"It would make me look small in all the pictures," frowned Mr. Nixon. "And Lindsay has that goddamn classic profile, whereas my nose is like a ski jump. And Lindsay has that gorgeous fair complexion. No *trace* even of five o'clock shadow. *Mine* begins to show as soon as I dry my face. Nothing would call attention to my blue pores and over-active follicles so fast as a running mate who has that goddamn pure Camay-soap Breck-girl complexion. Tell you what, gang. Let's put Lindsay on the back burner—"

"Gladly," said John Ehrlichman.

"—And maybe give him the double-o next time—for my second term, which we all better keep in mind in anything we consider doing!"

"Good thinking," said Mr. Haldeman.

"You're no dummy, Bob. I'm sure glad you came aboard!" Mr. Nixon turned to the pudgy-faced man who had been puffing on his pipe throughout. "John—I mean John *Mitchell,* not you, Dean—"

"Oh," said John Dean, who had leaped to his feet.

"—Who would make *you* happy, John, if you become my Attorney-General, as my running mate?"

"Nobody."

That was exactly what everyone had come to expect from John Mitchell: straight, curt, no-nonsense bluntness.

Mr. Nixon laughed. "That's pretty good, John—I mean John *Mitchell,* Dean. For *Chrissake* stop jumping up every time I mention a John.... That's a real zinger, John. 'Nobody!' Man, you sure lay it on the line. 'Nobody' would make you happy. Of course, nobody will make *me* entirely happy, too, to tell the straightforward truth. But let's be practical. We've got to have a candidate, John—*Mitchell!* Goddammit, Dean, leave the room! Go on. Get the hell out of here. You give me a pain in the ass with all that jumping up and ass-kissing."

John Dean left the room, ashen. "At this point in time?!" was heard echoing down the corridor.

"Dickie," said John (Mitchell), "I want to give it to you

straight. I don't care what anyone says: I don't think you should *have* a Vice President!"

A buzz of surprise and admiration rippled around the table.

"What the hell good is a Vice President, anyway?" asked John Mitchell. "He's only a stand-in, waiting like a ghoul for you to get knocked off so he can play the starring role!"

"True...." nodded Nixon.

"Vice Presidents always present a problem, *viz,* as we lawyers say: what the hell can you let them do without giving them too much publicity and building them up for 1972?"

"True!"

"So I say, to hell with it! We'll go with one man, not two. You, Dick. Nixon!"

"Why not put 'Nixon' on the polling ballots twice?" grinned a man whose name few in the room knew. The man was sitting in a corner, secretly fiddling with a tape-recorder, which was concealed in the cuspidor. The man's name was, I think, Liddy Gordon. 'Nixon-Nixon'! That's the ticket! Doubles your exposure. Demoralizes the Democrats. Will drive Larry O'Brien crazy."

"Let's run that up the flagpole and see who salutes it!" said earnest Bob Haldeman.

Only John Ehrlichman saluted.

Everyone laughed and a few loyal souls applauded. Senator Goldwater got his ten-gallon hat and started for the door. No one noticed this.

Mr. Nixon made a little temple of his hands. "That's an original and attractive idea, team. No two ways about it. No V.P.! Just two Presidents. Both me."

"It's not constitutional," Goldwater called from the doorway.

"What the hell has constitutionality to do with it?" barked Mr. Mitchell. "We're trying to win an election!"

"The Supreme Court won't stand for it," said Goldwater. "You've *got* to have a nominee for Vice President."

"Who says so?" bridled Mr. Mitchell.

"The Constitution says so!"

"No foolin'? I didn't know that."

Senator Goldwater closed the door.

"My mind is made up," said Mr. Nixon. "Barry was right. We've got to have a Vice President. No more stonewalling, fellows. No wagon trains around the White House."

"Not even bodies dangling in the breeze?" laughed Mr. Ehrlichman.

"Nope. Let me be absolutely clear about that, and to hell with the fate of the *lira*.... Let's get on with it! Recommendations?"

The recommendations resumed, with heightened feelings.

Someone suggested Ronald Reagan, and is doing nicely at the convalescent home. The next suggestions, though not in this order, were Walter Cronkite, David Eisenhower, and Abdul Kaminsky. Nixon rejected each name for a darn good reason. He had the hardest time dropping Kaminsky, who was half-Arab, half-Jewish, had married a Negress, and had been converted to Catholicism after twelve years as a Baptist choir boy. I don't have to tell you how hard it is for anyone with political savvy to turn down a man with such voter appeal. It was Maurice Stans who reminded Mr. Nixon that Abdul had served time in a Federal jug.

"For what?" asked Mr. Nixon.

"For poor penmanship."

"Since when is poor penmanship a federal crime?"

"Kaminsky was a forger, by profession."

That threw Kaminsky out of the running right then and there.

Things were getting nowhere, so Mr. Nixon turned to his most tried and trusted adviser: "Who do *you* recommend, dear?"

"We-el," said Mrs. Nixon, "when *I* go shopping, I consult the yellow pages."

The king-makers were electrified.

"Great Scott! What an idea!"

"Pat, you're a doozy!"

"A genius!"

"Get me a phone book! Goddammit, don't sit on your ass, Haldeman. Get me a Washington telephone directory!"

In no time at all, one of Mr. Haldeman's staff of experts had stolen a telephone book from the adjoining suite.

Swiftly, Nixon riffled the pages of the Classified Section to "VICE PRESIDENTS, AVAILABLE FOR." There, lo and behold, was one name: "Agnew, Spiro T."

"By God, there's a real pro!" exclaimed Mr. Nixon. "The only man in the whole goddamn Republican party with enough courage to advertise!" Mr. Nixon looked up. "Who is he?"

"Who?"

"Spiro Agnew."

The exchange had the perfect rhyme and cadence for a popular song, but no one knew Agnew, which is another appealing jingle.

Strom Thurmond said, "I *think* he's Mayor of South Dakota."

Julie Eisenhower said, "He'd have to be governor, Daddy. South Dakota is a state, not a city, so it takes a governor. *Cities* have mayors."

"Good thinking there," said Mr. Nixon.

"I'll be doggoned," said Ron Nessen.

"Can't you look this Agnew up in *Who's Who?*" asked Mrs. Nixon.

"Good thinking! Haldeman!"

This time Haldeman's squad had to ransack five suites before they could find a *Who's Who.* They found it by plumbing.

Nixon consulted the pantheon of self-inflation; and when he looked up at the others he was as pale as a Kabuki. "He's not in *Who's Who!*"

"What!"s, "Absurd!"s, "Impossible!"s swirled around that historic room. But it was not impossible. Look it up yourself: Spiro T. Agnew is not in *Who's Who: 1966–1968.*

"He *must* be somewhere in Miami," said Ray Bliss gloomily.

"He must of come to the convention, for Chrissake," said Charles Coulson, who was known to be religious.

"Man the telephones, gentlemen," snapped Mr. Nixon. "Everyone call a hotel."

"Or motel," added Mr. Mitchell. "Greeks like motels."

Well, my informants tell me they had a helluva hard time locating their man, because there are so many motels in Miami.

Luckily, the desk clerk at the Tahiti Turmoil said, "Ah, so. Here *is* an Agnew registered, and I rike him very much." The clerk was Japanese.

"Ring his room!" said Nixon.

"Agnew-san in Turkish bath."

"Page him!" thundered Nixon. "Even if he's in a Finnish sauna!"

"I give you honorable front desk."

They could all hear the Tahiti Turmoil's loudspeakers blaring, "Mr. Agnew.... Paging Spiro Agnew," in a Polish accent no one to this day can explain.

Now we cut to the steam room. A florid, dripping form lifted the phone. "Who? Oh. Well, which Spiro Agnew do you want? There are three of us in here."

"I want Spiro *T*. Agnew!" snapped Nixon.

"Oh, *that* Spiro Agnew," said Spiro P. Agnew. "I'll call him. Hey, Spiro T. It's for you."

A moment later, a damp voice said, "I don't *want* to see another slum! You've seen one, you've seen 'em all."

"Is this Governor Agnew?" asked Mr. Nixon.

"I think so," said Governor Agnew.

"What do you mean, you *think* so?"

"Well, it's pretty darn hot in here, hot shot. I feel dizzy.... Who's this?"

"*This* is Richard Nixon."

"Which Richard Nixon?"

"Your nominee for President, goddammit! Wait a minute. You *are* a Republican, aren't you?"

"Sure. There's no money in being a Democrat."

"Okay. That's all I need to know. *I want you to be my running mate!*"

"Why can't you exercise alone?"

"I want you to run *with,* not alongside, me," said Nixon in a very even tone.

"Where we gonna run?"

"We—are—going—to—run for the *Presidency* and *Vice* Presidency of the United States of—hello.... Hello?... Hello!... *Hello?!*"

That's how Spiro Agnew was chosen. Don't tell me you're surprised.

# 24

## A NOTE ON "COMMUNICATION"

ew words spark the imagination of contemporary social scientists—and of linguists, logicians, cybernetic Merlins, computer jockeys, mathematical wizards, "program" devisors, research planners, systems analysts—so swiftly as the thirteen-lettered rubric: "communication." Scarcely a field of investigation or invention today is uninfluenced by an awareness of the enormous potential of "the communication process." This virgin area has attracted many bright, young minds, and has been enthusiastically supported by philanthropic foundations. I daresay that the current catalogues of ninety percent of the colleges in the United States are peppered with courses on one or another aspect of those arenas of symbolic hopscotch spawned and sanctified under the portentous banner of "communications research."

It is not hard to see why this is so: only the unimaginative can quibble with the majestic payoffs which the analysis of communication promises—and has so richly demonstrated in so short a time.

In an earlier chapter, I said that we know almost nothing

about the process by which, every hour of the wakeful day, we all engage in the apparently mundane activity of trying to communicate with each other.

The problem of communication is expressed most simply in the situation of the human being trying to say something to another human being—with words, symbols, gestures, pictures—in an effort to get something from one head into another head.

The most delightful example I know of a totally discombobulating snafu in communication is this exchange of cables:

JAMSTONE
N.Y.
      SALES DISCUSSION FAILED. SHOULD I COME HOME OR RESUME BARGAINING?
                            HARPER

RALPH HARPER
LONDON
      YES.
                            JAMSTONE

JAMSTONE
N.Y.
      DO YOU MEAN STAY HERE OR COME HOME?
                            HARPER

RALPH HARPER
LONDON
      NO.
                            JAMSTONE

Of all human endeavors, communication is, it seems to me, uniquely imperfect. Science has invented symbols which are precise and mean the same thing to different people regardless of culture or background or psychological disposition.

Words do not do this.

The teacher of English is commonly believed to teach something called English. But the teacher of English tries to teach a *skill,* a method, a technique for the communication of three things: data, skills, ideas. We teach data quite well (even our lackadaisical seventh graders know there is a river called the Mississippi, an ocean known as the Atlantic, and that five plus one equals six). We teach skills fairly well (consider the number of people who can drive a car, change a washer, bake a cake, write a check). But we do not teach ideas anywhere as well as we should like to—because an astonishing number of people are incapable of handling abstractions.

Most people confuse confusion with profundity, and opaque prose with deep meaning. The teacher of English comes to understand that the study of English swiftly becomes a study of logic, a study of system, a study of order. It often attains the majesty of great mathematical equations, or great discoveries in science. And sometimes someone comes along, using the same words that have been used for generations, and puts them together in a way that lifts up the human race.

We have learned how intricate and subtle, how profoundly frustrating and multi-faceted, the process of communication is. The pioneering work in language of Sigmund Freud, Edward Sapir, Richard Lee Whorf, Noam Chomsky has cast electrifying light on the astonishing "parameters" which the "mundane" activity of communicating represents. The excitement generated by the first fumbling forays into the symbolic hall of mirrors hidden within the most primitive language, or the most ordinary sentence, began to infect physicists, philosophers, and engineers.

Before them, of course, the revolution called "symbolic logic," led by the work of Russell and Whitehead, and Rudolf Carnap, opened dazzling possibilities—which for a time remained unexploited. Then the genius of Norbert Wiener and Claude Shannon triggered an explosion of interest among the genies at Bell Laboratories and "think-tanks" around the world.

I am scarcely competent to comment on the theories of communication spouted by mathematicians or symbolic logicians, just as I am shamefully ignorant of the stupendous techniques involved in the construction of electronic calculators, circuitry "chips," the storage and retrieval of data, the scheme by which machines talk to machines.... But I think I can offer some observations about people talking to people, remarks which do not appear to have gained attention among the laity.

I believe there is a central impediment to communication: each of us has a certain amount of deep, stubborn *resistance to being communicated with*. Truly to listen to someone uttering more than banal thoughts can be—or seems to be—threatening. It means we are being asked to surrender control of the self; to entertain (at least) a challenge to those constructs in which we have invested considerable ego and emotion. New or radical ideas trip inner signals of warning, for ideas represent a danger which our unconscious or pre-conscious guardians against anxiety recognize. That danger involves the call upon us to surrender some portion of our precious autonomy.

It is obvious, empirically, that some people are much more successful than others in cozening us into listening. Some people are incomparably more effective than others in seducing us into a sense of reward or excitement about what they are saying. A superior teacher, writer, orator, demonstrably succeeds where others woefully fail. Why?

I am persuaded that the effective communicator is someone who first communicates (very rapidly) with himself and to himself. He conveys the feeling that it is *safe* to let him communicate with you. He creates a certain confidence that he knows what he is doing, in purpose and direction; that it is safe to put your fantasies in his hand; that it will all come out all right; that he is in confident control.

No more powerful words of communication have been invented by the human race than these four: "Once upon a time." This phrase, "Once upon a time," puts the listener into an accepting, receiving frame of mind. It says, "Remember? ... Don't worry. *I know what I'm doing.* I'm going to tell you a story...."

And there is a promise, in those magical four words, that five

others, familiar and consoling, will surely glorify the end: "...
they lived happily ever after."

I held forth on this theme in a lecture at Columbia twenty
years ago. Recently, I picked up with pricklings of *déja vu* the
new book by Bruno Bettelheim: *The Uses of Enchantment: The
Meaning and Importance of Fairy Tales.* With his customary insight and boldness, Bettelheim spells out the remarkable symbolic significance and lasting power of those tales we were read
in our childhood.

Fairy tales offer children reassuring solutions to the chaotic
anxieties and terrors which torment them. Each of us, in childhood, felt (correctly or not) that we were not understood (or
sufficiently appreciated) by our parents, that we were mistreated,
that we were bullied by older siblings or threatened by younger
ones upon whom our parents showered love which should have
gone to ourselves. This theme runs through all fairy tales—with
an ending that reassures the tender sensibilities of the children
to whom we read them.

The wicked characters in fairy tales are always punished. The
good (we) are unfailingly rewarded. The happy ending which
is a *sine qua non* of all fairy tales gives the child a priceless
promise—that he or she, too, truly understood, is virtuous and
deserving, and will "live happily ever after."

The frightening aspects of these stories, which make some
parents and teachers uneasy, and lead many to denounce Walt
Disney's rendition of the classics, may indeed frighten a child—
but can anyone doubt that children have (and would have) the
most terrifying fantasies even if they never heard of the wolf
who threatens to eat up Little Red Riding Hood, or the malevolent giant who would devour Jack of the Beanstalk? Children's
fantasies are packed with cackling witches and horrendous ogres.
Fairy tales assure the child that it *is not alone in being afraid,*
in feeling such terrors, and therefore need not feel a "coward"
—nor be ashamed.

The stories always move to a liberating catharsis and yearned-
for conclusion: Gretel burns the witch—in the very oven the

wicked creature intended to bake Gretel to death. Jack outwits the dreadful giant, and gets the golden goose and the magic harp. Little Red Riding Hood escapes the slathering wolf. As for Cinderella, just think of how those universal bogies of infancy—the jealous mother, cruel siblings—meet their doom because of their wicked and unjust treatment of sweet, innocent, mistreated Cinderella (me).

Much attention is paid, in contemporary research, to the communicator and his methods. Less, I believe, is paid to the communicatee. I have said that the communicator is uncommonly skilled in lowering and outflanking the anxious and obdurate defenses of the communicatee.

The communicatee, when properly courted and controlled, experiences the excitement of entering the unconscious world of someone else, of having his imagination freed, used, focused— and then returned to him safe.

We surrender our fantasies to those who are skilled enough to reassure us that they accept responsibility for the tension of uncertainty, and tacitly persuade us that that tension and uncertainty will be most happily dispelled.

The effective communicator must have a capacity for *multiple identifications.* By that I mean he changes his effort according to his prescience about the effects upon one listener as against another. The skillful communicator identifies with whomever he is talking to or writing for. He tests out the effect of his words upon the identifying part of himself. This means that he must be able to carry on, with electronic speed, an *internal dialogue* in which his listener or reader is encapsulated and in which he, the communicator, first tries out within himself alternative ways of bridging the gap between himself and another.

I have long admired J. Irwin Miller of the Cummins Engine Company in Indiana, to whom I once listened in a television panel discussion of some political problem. His fellow panelists, card-carrying Highbrows, treated Mr. Miller with either condescension or forbearance, since it was clear that he was that most ludicrous of types: a Businessman. The Deep Thinkers savaged points Mr. Miller never made and ridiculed policies he had never propounded.

Finally, Mr. Miller, who was not at home with the ploys of Academe, said, "In my home, I have taught my children: you can disagree with a person's position as much as you want to—*after* you have been able to state it to his satisfaction."

I consider this one of the most sagacious feats of analysis of a basic requirement in communication.

I have always believed that good style in writing rests on clear thinking. So does clear teaching or talking or lecturing. It is a striking, lamentable truth that most people spray out a large number of sounds in speech, or scribbles in writings, and hope that something will somehow happen to convey something—somehow. But the good communicator always makes himself clear *to himself* before he tries to make himself clear to others. He knows that very rare thing: what he really wants to say.

This seductive puzzle, communication, exists in the paint on a canvas, in the symbols of the mathematician, in the models of the scientists, in the interrelations of human beings who try to escape their own loneliness, to share experience, to communicate feelings—feelings which are common to the human race, yet different in each of us and very difficult to convey as we would like to.

Communication is a problem in creating techniques by which we can be understood. We need not hope to be agreed with; it is miracle enough to be really understood.

## THE GREAT BERLIN CAPER

**E**very January thirtieth, my mind goes back to one of the most fantastic episodes of my life. It was November, 1942—a year after Pearl Harbor. Our world could hardly have looked more awful. Hitler had conquered Europe, from the Atlantic to the Black Sea.

I was in the Office of War Information. Washington was being bombarded with propaganda ideas from geniuses in New York and Hollywood and most of the terrain in between. Some of the brainstorms were imaginative, even ingenious; but their chief *effect*, had they been executed, would only have been to make their proponents feel better. It is remarkable how few people possess an objective sense of objective consequence.

On one committee in the capital, my opposite number, representing Britain, was David Bowes-Lyon, brother of the then-Queen. He was very handsome, charming, impeccably tailored. He conducted himself with that air of confidence and amusement that is the special style of the English aristocrat. When he offered an idea, it was with an apologetic air—and a twinkle of the eye that belied it.

We were discussing the forthcoming January 30 (1943), on which date the Nazis would celebrate ten years in power. (Hindenburg had given Hitler the keys to the safe at 11 A. M., January 30, 1933.) And January 30, by gruesome coincidence, was President Roosevelt's birthday. Goebbels would surely put on a propaganda orgy, broadcasting Nazi triumphs to the captive French and Poles and Czechs and Norwegians and Danes.... The world's press and radio would have to carry every boast Hitler and his litter uttered; not until the next day could editors and columnists in the free world answer the lies.

"The Nazis," someone said, "will force the entire Continent to listen. They have loudspeakers in all the public squares and big factories."

"Quite," said David Bowes-Lyon.

I winced.

We contemplated the prospects glumly.

"If," I ventured dreamily, "you could please bomb Berlin at eleven A.M. on January 30—"

"I beg your pardon?"

"—and force the Berlin off the air—"

"In the *day*time?" David murmured. "We've never done that."

"—we could have standby programs ready—in English, German, French, Dutch. So if Radio Berlin goes blank, people will fiddle with their dials—" I was winging it in my daydream. "—and they'll pick up *our* broadcasts on the same theme: 'Ten years of Nazism.' No political sermons, David, just straightforward appeal: 'Where were you ten years ago? Where was your husband? Your brother? Your son? Think—' "

In a burst of British enthusiasm, David said, "Mmhhh. . . ."

I did not see him for four or five days—until he drifted into my office and said, "Our chaps will do it."

"Do what?"

"Bomb Berlin. Eleven A.M. January thirtieth."

I kept myself from fainting, then gulped, "But how do you know?"

"I was just there," he said with a pained air. "London. Flew over right after our meeting. Talked to Bracken, Winston's man—

and Winston approved. *Much* pleased.... Our chaps think it could be a good show. Mosquitos—swift aircraft, made of plywood—will go in, low-level, hit Berlin, and hurry home."

And they did.

On January thirty-first, British and American headlines ran: DAYLIGHT RAID ON BERLIN! BBC broadcast the news to all of occupied Europe.

Royal Air Force planes had knocked Radio Berlin off the air just after *Reichsmarschall* Hermann Goering had begun the historic address. (Hitler had a throat ailment, and did not orate as planned.) The sound of bombs *exploding in the Wilhelmstrasse* had been clearly heard over Europe's radios!

I heard it all on recordings myself, later—on recordings made in London and flown to Washington: the opening fanfare of trumpets; the proud roll of drums; the haughty voice of an announcer: "*Meine Damen und Herren...Reichsmarschall Hermann Goering!*" Goering's voice. A few words—then, an explosion. Muffled. Then another. Confusion erupted in the studio. Cries of consternation; shouts of surprise; the barking of orders; German voices yelling, "Start over!" "Begin again!"

Again the trumpets blasted, again the drums rolled, again the announcer introduced Hermann Goering, again Goering started —and now the bombs exploded nearer, louder, and suddenly the rattle of German antiaircraft fire came on!

Panic in the studio. Shouts. Curses. Chairs pushed over. A voice screamed, "Cut off! Get off!"

Then: silence. The most beautiful silence I ever heard.... And I knew that transmitters in London and in our undercover mobile vans and trucks around Europe (laundry trucks, plumbing trucks, moving vans) were broadcasting *our* version of the Dark Decade.

After V-E Day, I was sent to Paris. One mellow afternoon I found myself with André, a hero of the Resistance, at a café table on the Champs-Élysées. He was a short, inconspicuous man with sardonic eyes. He was badly scarred and walked with a bad limp. His left arm was immobilized. The scars, the limp, the arm were mementos of Gestapo torture. He had been arrested and imprisoned many times.

We talked until the pink twilight fell. He told me—quite calmly—some of the things he had endured. I shivered.

"But how could you go on?" I asked. "Where did you get the —spirit?"

He shrugged. "Ah, you have not lived under the Boche. There was no *choice* except to hate them and fight them. Even with bare hands."

"But France fell in '40. It was four *years* before we invaded Normandy. What kept you going?"

"Oh, sometimes a thing would happen: a sign of hope. *Par exemple,* I was working in the Renault plant, where they made tanks. I was making sabotage, spoiling parts. Came one day— eleven o'clock, January 30. All work stopped. We must stand by our machines and listen to a speech. From Berlin. From Hermann Pig Goering himself. For the tenth anniversary of Nazism! ... *Alors!* First we hear the drums and trumpets. Then Goering starts." André's eyes glittered. "Then—*mon Dieu!* Bombs. Bombs! Falling on Berlin?! Yes! In the daytime! Yes! ... We heard the bombs!

"The Nazis are running around in that radio studio frantic, shouting orders, and again—boom-boom-*boom!* ... And poof! Off goes all sound! Silence. ...

"We realize what has happen! A tremendous cheer—again and again—in the factory. We know a turning point has arrived. The Boche are not invincible! *Berlin itself bombed!* The plant guards run around and strike blows on us with sticks, and the machines begin again, we must resume work. ... But it was never again as before. We knew now the Allies could win."

He glanced toward the Arc de Triomphe, cream and mauve in the dying sun. "That was an immense event. ... The underground was ecstatic. ... How explain it? To bomb Berlin—at the precise hour of celebrating. ... Our operatives in Germany soon sent word to us about it." He laughed. "This Goebbels, this club-foot monster, he choked, he screamed, he blamed Goering,

Germany's air defense—and what do you think he said? 'This raid was not the *Englander*'s idea! No, no. This is the trick of some damn American bastard—to break our anniversary, to give Jew Roosevelt a present for his birthdate!'" He paused. "Did Washington know this?"

I sipped some cognac. "No," I said.

# 26

---

## SERMON:
### Madness in Academe

DEARLY BELOVED:

We live in times so violent, so irrational, so ominous, so confused and confusing that this sermon will fall upon many a deaf or derisive ear.

We stand in peril of being stampeded by the over-simplifier, however honest; the fanatic, however idealistic; the unstable, however eloquent; and the naive, however appealing. Nietzsche warned us of an appalling truth: "Fanatics are picturesque—and the human race prefers admiring poses to listening to reason."

The glittering nostrums of spellbinders have proved so disastrous in this century, and have taken so monstrous a toll in human lives and freedom, that only fools or zealots can rush to repeat both the gullibility and the horrors. Must each generation learn for itself that virtue does not solve equations? That ideology is blind? That when altruists turn militant they become self-righteous tyrants?

Many noble-minded reforms fail because of the subterranean

complexity of our problems; others, because of our God-given inability to attain omniscience.

I hasten to add, for the benefit of those who read and run (or riot), that "solutions" to problems much simpler than ours have proven disastrous failures in Socialist heavens—Russia, China, Poland, Cuba, emerging Africa.

Whenever I find myself touched by the blazing sincerity of young people, by their shining ideals and compassion, by their discontent with the undeniable evils and injustices of this sorry world, I am brought up short by their naive and reckless prescriptions. At such moments, a line from H. L. Mencken flares in my memory: "An idealist is someone who, upon observing that a rose smells better than a cabbage, concludes that it will also make better soup."

I hope you will one day realize that the doctrinaire are far more dangerous than the cynical. Throughout man's history, no group has done more harm, shed more blood, caused more tragedy than those who, sincerely ignorant, added passion to their certitudes. That is what I fear most about sincere youth.

> Young people have exalted notions, because they have not yet been humbled by life or learned its necessary limitations.... They would always rather do noble deeds than useful ones: their lives are regulated by moral feeling more than by reasoning.... All their mistakes are in the direction of doing things excessively and vehemently.... They love too much, hate too much. They think they know everything; this, in fact, is why they overdo everything.

This cleansing passage is from Aristotle's *Rhetorica*.

When the explosion of violence convulsed our campuses, in that decade historians may well, in their bewilderment, call The Crazy Era, my generation was caught between the opposed pulls of sympathy for their children and horror of their rampages.

And as the rebellion gained strength, we tasted the poison of demagogues, vandals, terrorists, bombers, blackmailers, hooligans, invading agitators who were neither students nor teachers.

It became clearer and clearer that a generation of college students had become mesmerized by articulate bubbleheads purveying political hallucinations. And when classrooms were invaded by chain-swinging hoodlums, when buildings were burned, deans beaten, non-political students maimed or killed by ill-timed bombs, the words of Winston Churchhill should have illuminated the moral landscape: "I cannot remain impartial as between the fire and the fire brigade."

Clarity was finally forced upon the parents and professors of that ghastly time. We had no *right* to bargain away the precious civil rights we had inherited. We had no *right* to bribe bullies, appease extremists, propitiate temper-tantrums. We had no right to surrender to the infantile and the paranoid.

We had no right to be cowards.

We had no right to sell or subvert or abandon the citadels of what, for all its ethical faults and economic imperfections, is still man's last, best hope on earth.

In a commencement address at Northwestern, Professor Bergen Evans began with a striking suggestion to the graduating commandoes:

> ...steal a furtive glance behind you. You will see some of the most remarkable people ever to inhabit the earth—your parents and grandparents.
>
> For these are the people who, within five or six decades, have increased life expectancy by approximately fifty percent; who have eradicated plagues; who cut the working day by a third [and] doubled real wages. These are the people who, building thousands of high schools and colleges, have made higher education—once a privilege of the few—available to many millions.
>
> These are the people who, without bloodshed, effected, in 1930, a social revolution which in its humane consequences makes the French Revolution seem a mere outburst of savagery and the Russian Revolution a political retrogression.

These are the people who established the United Nations, who defeated Hitler, contained Stalin, and made Khrushchev back down.

These are the people who, after spending billions on prosecuting a war, gave billions more, not only to their friends but even to their former enemies, so that the world would not plunge into a devastating depression.

These are the people who soared outward into space... and downward into the atom, releasing for man's use... the primal energy of the cosmos.

And while doing all this, they produced a great literature and an exciting architecture—indeed, stimulated extraordinary experimentation and creativity in all the arts. (June 14, 1969)

It is, of course, unrealistic to expect the young to realize all that this means. It is small wonder that the early heralds of youth's passion, e.g., Paul Goodman, perhaps even Herbert Marcuse and Charles Reich, find themselves disillusioned, chastened, and ignored by the flock whose cause they romantically championed.

One professor, who was quick to join one of the earliest campus crusades, has said with some bitterness that it is absurd to expect the young to offer solutions to any of the problems about which they riot. It is a pity the professor had to learn what a seventy-two-year-old Druse farmer said to an interviewer:

> If you give a child responsibility, he will ruin you. He is not prudent... he doesn't know what to do. He doesn't know how to spend the money and how to do his work. So I will not agree to give away authority. I feel that I am wiser than my children; so I have to keep this responsibility.*

I am constantly surprised by the malarkey people accept as undisputed truth. It is asserted, *ad nauseum,* that a "growing

---

* See Joseph Adelson, *The New York Times,* January 18, 1970.

percentage of our population is aged fourteen to twenty-five."
This is very significant; it is also very wrong.

The young are growing in numbers; but their *proportion* in
the total population still stands around 20 percent of the total.
The median age in America in 1910 was twenty-four. Today it
is twenty-seven years eight months. Population experts expect it
to be around twenty-eight in 1985. We are getting *older,* not
younger; there are more of us, and more who live longer, than
ever before.

What *has* zoomed fantastically is the number of young who
go to high school and college. Since 1950, high-school enrollment has more than doubled; college enrollment has tripled.

Over seven million (!) students in America today cramp
our colleges: Seven million equals the combined populations of
Rotterdam, Stockholm, Dublin, Belgrade, Liverpool, Oakland,
Des Moines, Norway, and Iceland.

The magnitude of the repercussions of this number is only
beginning to be comprehended. I, for one, do not believe there
are seven million high-school graduates in the United States
who really want to go to college—to be educated. Their parents
may push them to. And our affluence has made them economi-
cally obsolete: They have nothing else to do. (Virtuous Minimum Wage laws serve to bar many from working.)

If there are too many students in college, there also are too
many who are too old to be treated as children. Our young today
mature physically at a younger age than their grandparents did
(the onset of menstruation, for instance, has dropped six months
each decade). We forget that the idea of the college acting as
parent dates back to the time when college students *were* children: As late as the eighteenth century, college freshmen were
thirteen and fourteen years old. It is silly to subject a returned
soldier, or a twenty-one-year-old girl devirgined in the eighth
grade, to parietal regulations.

It is interesting that the students who complained most about
too large classes, and being "robbed of identity," and being
"mere numbers in an impersonal computer operation," never-

theless continued to prefer the huge, overloaded colleges. Why? Because the large schools are more interesting, more challenging, more rewarding, and offer more choices. The smaller colleges, with one faculty member for each fifteen students, lose applicants (and honor students) to schools where the student population is greater than many townships. Branches of the University of California which are small, attractive, comforting, set in salubrious locations, have for years had difficulty attracting students, who continue to prefer the "impersonal" big caldron of Berkeley.*

We may console ourselves with the awareness that certain problems are not ours alone, nor the product of American family indulgences or deficiencies, nor—above all—the bitter fruits of a "heartless business of civilization."

> Old men have assured me, in Mayan, in Navajo and in Arabic, that the young are lazy and self-indulgent, that they are given over to smoking, peyote-eating or drunkenness, that they do not uphold the important traditions, and that they are the spoilt children of affluence: "Life is easier now and so they do not want to work."†

Adolescence is an entirely new phenomenon in human society. (Puberty is another matter.) Adolescence is the product of modern, relatively affluent society—since, say, 1910. Before that, young men (and some young women) went to work around the age of fourteen. It would have been thought inconceivable that millions upon millions of the young would be prevented from doing anything useful, even during the long summer months when schools, for obsolete agricultural reasons, are closed. (Farmers' children were needed to bring in the crop.)

The most neglected aspect of student revolt in America was the support it received from members of the faculty. They lent

---

* From Seymour Martin Lipset in *Daedalus*, Winter, 1970.
† David Gutman, *New York Times*, sp. supp., January 12, 1970.

rebellion their names, their encouragement, their speeches—and gave them money for the furtherance of the cause. "Some eminent, powerful, internationally seasoned and immensely prestigious faculty... served the students well. Most of them later fled to other campuses or retreated behind locked Institute doors, but in the beginning they served the student revolutionists well."*

In the balances of history, I think greater honor will be accorded teachers such as the young one who wrote this:

> Whether we like it or not, by becoming teachers we accept important power over the lives of students; accordingly, we have to be ready to show, when push becomes shove, that we have personal integrity to match that power.
>
> The generation gap in the universities begins in ourselves as teachers... in the gap between our own pretensions to intellectual leadership and our willingness to pay the price of the power that we seek.†

I wonder how those faculty members who aided campus revolt will come to terms with themselves in a calmer future. Did they not give away rights they would have refused to surrender to, say, an investigating committee of Congress, or a reactionary board of trustees, or a witch-hunting press? Did they not ask the law to close its eyes to actions they would never have defended had mobs come to the colleges from a construction site? Did they not provide excitable, immature students with the invaluable rationalization that violations of peace and law are moral, indeed admirable, once worthy slogans are mouthed? Did they not ask for amnesty for acts committed on a campus which, if committed by their enemies—or in their neighborhood —they would have denounced with horror? Did they ask themselves what was the effect on the America beyond the college

---

* Robert Nisbet, *Encounter,* February, 1970.
† David Gutman, *op. cit.*

gates of making a campus a sanctuary for lawbreaking and an inviolable base, a "neutral" staging ground, for hit-and-run guerrilla raids off-campus? Did they not see what was plain to see: that the extremist Left is certain to provoke a frightening response from the extremist Right? Did they not understand that a revolution does not long shelter ecstasy or mass hysterias? Did they not see that persistent "confrontations" with the power structure are sooner or later bound to force police powers to be exercised? Were they really ready to accept Mao's dicta: "Power grows out of the barrel of a gun.... A revolution is not a tea party?" Did they think rioting a spectator sport? Had they no guilt about students who were beaten, teachers who were vilified, lecturers who were shouted down by neo-Nazi mob chantings? Had they no doubts when colleagues' offices were sacked, their manuscripts destroyed, their homes desecrated with painted obscenities, their families terrorized by telephoned threats of murder? Did they shrug off as lamentable, "to be expected," or "sick" the making and planting of bombs by students who had been led to believe that extreme means are justified by noble ends?

What absurdity it is to call the university repressive or intolerant, a tool of sinister conspiracy, the enemy of progress and peace, the stifler of unorthodox ideas. It is academic freedom and academic tenure that allow the charges to thrive and proliferate until they verge on what can only be called paranoia. I know of no instructor, teacher, or professor who complained that he could not teach or think or say or write what he believed. I know of no student who can truthfully say that he cannot read or write or say anything he chooses to.

The larger irony, which makes Right-wingers see red (in more ways than one), is that it is precisely the American colleges that have been the most prolific producers of free, unorthodox, radical ideas and leaders. The colleges were at the very center of the peace movement. The anti-Vietnam pressures began on our campuses and in national student and faculty sit-ins and teach-ins. The opposition to the draft was emphatically launched in our colleges. At Columbia, a poll of both the undergraduate and graduate faculties found that seventy percent favored America's withdrawal from Vietnam when the rest of the population supported President Johnson.

I wonder how decent men, whatever the accident of their color, can defend, say, the Special Co-ordinator of Black Studies at San Francisco State College, Mr. Nathan Hare, who, according to the local press, said in a public speech:

> They say we are too few to fight. We should vote. But I can kill twenty [white] men. I can cut one's throat, shoot another, drop a hand grenade in the middle of a whole bunch. I get only a single vote, and that's between the lesser of the two evils.... I don't believe in absolutes, so I do not categorically reject all white men—only 99 and 44/100th of them.

How can serious men so confuse the issue of authority (not power) in a university? Students come to college because they lack knowledge. Can they possibly be competent to decide what they should learn, or how it should be taught, or by whom? The goal of those who teach is to go on teaching—that is, to stay in colleges; the goal of most students is to leave, the sooner the better.

How can one defend college quotas on an ethnic or racial basis? A quota that favors any group must, sooner or later, operate at the expense of another group. The most impressive academic performance by groups (to those who insist on thinking that way) is made by Chinese, Jewish, and Japanese students. Shall seven out of ten be asked, or forced, to leave? Or has "America known enough of anti-Semitism and anti-Oriental feeling to be wary of opening that box again." Is not the problem to widen, not lower, the area of eligibility, without reference to color or creed, and without the introduction of criteria that are extraneous to education? How bitter is the paradox of liberals who, a decade ago, fought the practice of requiring college applicants to submit a photograph (which permitted discrimination against skin color or nose shapes or eye slantings), but today support the practice—because "How else can you identify the blacks?"*

My sense of astonishment is not limited to the campus. Consider the spectacle of the theorist of radical feminists, Ti-Grace Atkinson, addressing a conference of two hundred women, brought together by the State of New York's Women's Unit, of Governor Nelson Rockefeller's office and the National Conference of Christians and Jews. The liberating ladies applauded when Ti-Grace Atkinson urged them to "support the prostitute.... Go out on the street to help her.... The prostitute is the only honest woman left in America... because they charge for their services, rather than submitting to a marriage contract which forces them to work for life without pay."†

Nor does my sense of astonishment diminish when I read the editorials in dyed-in-the-blue organs of the Establishment. In the midst of a rash of bomb explosions and bomb scares, *The New York Times* editorialized: "Bombings must not be glossed over as the actions of idealistic if misguided revolutionaries; they are the criminal acts of potential murderers." The potential murderers in New York included some students who had made Columbia a shambles, were martyred, by some members of the press, as pure victims of a brutal and repressive society, and were no doubt encouraged to extend their intransigent idealism to a monstrous conclusion. Another newspaper crisply noted:

When members of the cultural elite feel a need to remind each other that bombers are not idealists, we can see that those who should be guarding the bonds have been tearing them down.‡

I was mystified when friends who should have known better denounced the proposed building, by Columbia, of an $11,000,000 gymnasium, a proposal first made by the City of

---

* John Bunzel, *The Public Interest,* Fall, 1968.
† *The New York Times,* March 13, 1970.
‡ *Wall Street Journal,* March 23, 1970.

New York in 1959, which *fifty-nine percent of the Harlem community had approved.* Mark Rudd and his guerrillas, who clearly had no interest in the gym but were hell-bent on committing *some* destructive act against Columbia, succeeded in stopping construction of the gymnasium. The muggings and thefts and terrorism on the site increased at a rate frightening to the residents, black or white, on Morningside Drive. It had been one of the purposes of the new gymnasium to reduce crime in the area through the daily presence and movement of students.

> The worst effect of student violence has been to excite liberals who assume that behind every act of violence there is a condition of injustice, and who take it as their guilty responsibility to eradicate the cause.*

Those who encourage the militant young tell them that they are a new elite, the honest, uncorrupted ones who will abolish evil and injustice where previous men have failed. I cannot see why or how some special insight or superior wisdom proceeds automatically from being under twenty-five. Idealism *is* a common property of youth, but it is far from restricted to the young. Nor is idealism, in the young or the old, necessarily paired with judgment or knowledge, or competence or plain sense. If patriotism, as Samuel Johnson said, is the refuge of scoundrels, then idealism is too often the refuge of ignorance.

I cannot help thinking that much of the student movement rested on the drive for immediate, undeterred gratification of the senses. Anything that thwarts the whim of the moment is called "repressive." That such unbridled hedonism, at the expense of work, study, discipline, or knowledge, should be hailed as "liberating" strikes me as tragic.

How rash to call this generation "the brightest, best-educated generation in history." It cannot be the brightest, since intelligence is a constant proportion and, for the most part, is inherited; and it cannot be the best-educated, considering the

---

* William Letwin, in *The Public Interest*, Fall, 1969.

scandalous proportion of our young who cannot write well, who have not read the classics, who cannot pass an elementary examination in history, economics, any science, philosophy, political theory. Let teachers over forty contradict me.

I never forgot Bruno Bettelheim's account of the famous congregation of music lovers at Woodstock:

> And (I) heard the same stories that you got from the March on Washington—how wonderful that somebody shared his blanket with me; somebody shared his food with me; we had a wonderful time, we sat up all night, sang all night, drank all night....
>
> Youth has a tremendous need to get together in large groups, to get intoxicated by the image of each other's presence. I cannot be too impressed by the external forms because I see the underlying need, which is the same—to escape loneliness, my isolation; to find reaffirmation that I am a worthwhile person in the fact that so many other people do the same things I do.*

One of the principal victims of the storm that had swept our campuses is the sense of history, a continuing appraisal of the past and its meaning, a charting of where we were and where we are and where we can (or should) be heading. History is not a barren chronicle of dates and names; it is the retracing of human problems, those efforts, errors, successes by which we may have some context within which to think and judge, some light to guide our search for causes and effects, some signals of warning, some tested beacons with which to light our voyage toward a wider, deeper humaneness.

Even a passing knowledge of that Pandora's box in which are treasures called Justice, Freedom, Equality, Peace, Security— and poisons such as Poverty, Prejudice, Irrationality, Killing, Hate—even a surface knowledge, I say, must lower the mature man's expectations of the imminence of a millennium.

---

* *New York Times Magazine*, January 11, 1970.

The agitated think that money or legislation, fervor or evangelism can swiftly set things right. But the men who know most (I am not among them), the men who have studied with care what we presently do know about a given field or conflict or policy, will agree with Daniel Bell:

> That political liberalism is in crisis is quite true, but perhaps not for reasons given by the student Left—in fact, for reasons that would not be to its liking. For if there is a single source for the crisis of liberalism—apart from the Vietnam War—it is the complexity of our social problems, the linked nature of change, and a lack of knowledge (or adequate research) about where and how one can effectively "cut into the system" in order to direct social change. The old simplifications about "more" schools and "more" housing, or even "better" schools or "better" housing, have not proved very useful in breaking the cycle of poverty or in dealing with Negro family structure. For those given to moralisms or "sophisticated" chatter about "power," such talk about complexities is irritating... they regard it as an evasion of the "real" problem.*

This is a bitter lesson to learn; and the young, as I and my friends in the Thirties, resent and resist and deny it. I can only urge today's crusaders for justice to reflect for a moment on the fact that not *all* of the unhappy are right. Not *every* grievance is justified. Not *every* inequity proves that a malevolent society caused it. And not every hammer means that something needs smashing.

Democracy *is* a slow, troublesome, frustrating, hazardous way of trying to solve persistent human problems. It shows us all its baffling ailments: injustice and insufficiency, corrupt men and debased methods, fitful disorders and fevers, and that impassioned disputation that frightens those who have not learned that the hottest arguments take place within the family.

---

* *Daedalus,* Winter, 1970.

The [democratic] public is constantly reminded, in the most vivid way, of the evils in its own society and in those other countries where television is free to prowl. But the evils of life in closed totalitarian countries cannot be given anything like the same emphasis. All of which tends to lead to a grossly distorted view of the world.*

The rebellious young, whose dissent and protest deserve the highest respect (just as their virulence and violence do not), are part and parcel of that way of ordering our lives that makes it possible for us to grow, to invent, to improve—without censorship, blackmail, force, or fraud.

It was Whitehead, I think, who said:

The art of free society consists, first, in the maintenance of the symbolic code; and secondly, in fearlessness of revision.... Those societies which cannot combine reverence to their symbols with freedom of revision, must ultimately decay....

Where, then, do I end? With a sense of sorrow that a polemical tract such as this is necessary in the seventh decade of the twentieth century. With the conviction that words do matter, and ideas do count, and debate is imperative. With a plea to those who use violence—whether in deeds or slogans—to consider the carnage and chaos they may bring down upon themselves, and us.

Senator Margaret Chase Smith made a prediction I would urge the young to read with care:

Extremism... is increasingly forcing upon the American people the narrow choice between anarchy and repression. And make no mistake about it, if that narrow choice has to be made, the American people, even if with reluctance and misgiving, will choose repression.

Ironically, the excesses of dissent in the extreme left

* Robin Day, *Encounter*, May, 1970.

can result in repression of dissent. For repression is preferable to anarchy and nihilism to most Americans.

It is time that the greater center of our people, those who reject the violence and unreasonableness of both the extreme right and extreme left, searched their consciences, mustered their moral and physical courage, shed their intimidated silence, and declared their consciences.

How do I close? With the certainty that nothing is more sacred than the uncompromising pursuit of truth, whomever it may disappoint or contradict or upset. With a renewed commitment to the surpassing miracle of a society in which men are free—even to extol folly, or mock experience, or pursue false gods, or say things that make me shiver. Consider this concluding passage from Edgar Z. Friedenberg's sprightly article "The Generation Gap":

> If the confrontation between the generations does pose, as many portentous civic leaders and upper-case "Educators" fear, a lethal threat to the integrity of the American social system, that threat may perhaps be accepted with graceful irony. Is there, after all, so much to lose? The American social system has never been noted for its integrity. In fact, it would be rather like depriving the Swiss of their surfing.*

The frivolity of the simile makes me shudder. If the American social system "has never been noted for its integrity" it has certainly been noted for suffering and supporting professors who publish such irresponsible bile.

Democracy, and only democracy, has structured power in such a way that social change can proceed legally, peacefully, without the horrors of purges, the insanities of fanaticism, the suffocating imposition of dogma. This tormented century has driven home more forcefully than ever the lesson that that nation will prove most enduring which is most resilient, most

---

* Annals of the American Academy of Political and Social Science, March, 1969.

moderate, most just, most adjustable to the inevitable strains and pains that accompany social change. Freedom of criticism, freedom of argument, freedom for the unorthodox to challenge the prevailing consensus is still the first and final bastion free men must defend.

To such men, fear is a poor response to delirium. The English journal *The Spectator* remarked:

> The threat of the universities lies not from the students, but from the reactions of the authorities. By pandering to the student "leaders," by treating the game as if it were much more than a game, the university authorities run two risks. The first ... is that they will encourage the popular backlash against public spending on university education. Few ordinary people, as it is, have much time for the spurious grievances of what they see as a pampered minority. The student leaders may succeed in "radicalizing" their middle-class contemporaries; they are succeeding even better in "conservatising" the proletariat.
>
> But the second and far greater danger is that, because they lack the confidence to defend the institutions they are meant to lead, and the liberal values those institutions are meant to represent, they will by their own actions destroy the universities and everything they stand for. If a whiff of the Weimar republic lies over Britain today, it is not difficult to discern where the blame lies. Not with the students or self-styled enemies of the established order, but with the guardians, both in the universities and elsewhere, of the most precious institutions of our civilization, who have lost the will and the self-confidence to fulfill their trust. (March 7, 1970)

The only force I fear more than human irrationality is irrationality armed with passion. It is endemic to our common, many-colored race. Perhaps these words will help reduce unreason's malignant growth.

*Your most humble servant,*
LEO ROSTEN